PRAISE FOR SOLOMON AND THE ANT

"This is a conversation between the Qur'an and the Bible as serious as it is simple. Applying a wealth of scholarly experience, Penchansky engages the holy texts both thematically and thoughtfully. Using his mastery of post-biblical and Islamic traditions, the author ensures a robust discussion about how readers wrestle with God through the stories of scripture."

—EMRAN EL-BADAWI, UNIVERSITY OF HOUSTON

"Some of the most obscure Qur'anic passages that seem to discuss fantastical realms, such as the *jinn* or demons, speaking animals, magical worlds of angels or deities, and mystical journeys have no recognizable biblical counterparts. Yet Penchansky is so well-versed in biblical literature that he brings a genuine voice artfully and skillfully mirroring Qur'anic narratives with similitudes in biblical literature. Away from any polemics, this is brilliantly an honest and sympathetic reflection that would undoubtedly enlighten and enrich any reader of the Qur'an."

—ABDULLA GALADARI, KHALIFA UNIVERSITY OF SCIENCE AND TECHNOLOGY

"This book makes a unique and important contribution to the study of the relationship between the Bible and the Qur'an. Adopting a thematic approach, Penchansky offers a set of insightful and creative studies that explore how the two texts address the topics of polytheism, theodicy, and revelation. Readers will come away with a deeper appreciation of the fascinating interconnections that exist between the scriptures of the monotheistic traditions."

—JOHN KALTNER, RHODES COLLEGE

"The Qur'an's narrative extension of the biblical tradition has been the subject of much scholarly discussion. While most scholars who engage in this field are trained in Qur'anic studies, Penchansky's training in the Hebrew Bible makes *Solomon and the Ant* an important and unique contribution. Through a careful analysis of parallel stories in the Bible and the Qur'an, this book demonstrates how the two scriptures share the same cultural milieu, without losing sight of the Qur'an's theological peculiarity, and it does so with commendable clarity."

—MUN'IM SIRRY, AUTHOR OF *CONTROVERSIES OVER ISLAMIC ORIGINS*

Solomon and the Ant

Solomon and the Ant

The Qur'an in Conversation with the Bible

DAVID PENCHANSKY

CASCADE *Books* · Eugene, Oregon

SOLOMON AND THE ANT
The Qur'an in Conversation with the Bible

Unless otherwise indicated, I use this Qur'anic translation: A. J. Droge, trans. *The Qur'an: A New Annotated Translation*. Sheffield: Equinox, 2013.

Cascade Books
An Imprint of Wipf and Stock Publishers
199 W. 8th Ave., Suite 3
Eugene, OR 97401

www.wipfandstock.com

PAPERBACK ISBN: 978-1-7252-8868-3
HARDCOVER ISBN: 978-1-7252-8869-0
EBOOK ISBN: 978-1-7252-8870-6

Cataloguing-in-Publication data:

Names: Penchansky, David, author.

Title: Solomon and the ant : The Qur'an in conversation with the Bible / David Penchansky.

Description: Eugene, OR: Cascade Books, 2021. | Includes bibliographical references and index.

Identifiers: ISBN 978-1-7252-8868-3 (paperback). | ISBN 978-1-7252-8869-0 (hardcover). | ISBN 978-1-7252-8870-6 (ebook).

Subjects: LCSH: Qur'an—Criticism, interpretation, etc. | Qur'an—Relation to the Bible. | Polytheism—Islam. | Good and evil—Religious aspects—Islam. | Revelation—Islam.

Classification: BP134.B4 P300 2021 (print). | BP134 (ebook).

07/19/21

Dedicated to my longtime brothers,
David Barnes, Fr. Richard Vettel-Becker,
Turner Collins, and Don McSpaddon

Contents

Introduction

What's so special about the Qur'an? Muslims believe their sacred book consists of the actual words of God in Arabic, dictated to the Prophet Muhammad by the angel Gabriel. How does one examine such a claim, which goes beyond what most Jews and Christians believe about their holy texts? The Qur'an claims that its divine nature will be obvious to anyone who reads it with an open heart. These are some Qur'anic texts that make this claim:[1]

> If you are in doubt about what We have sent down to Our servant, then bring a sura [chapter] like it, and call your witnesses. (Q 2:23)

> Or do they say, "He has forged it?" Say: "Then bring ten suras forged like it, and call on whomever you can, other than God, if you are truthful." (Q 11:13)

> Say: "If indeed humankind and the jinn joined together to produce something like this Qur'an, they would not produce anything like it, even if they were supporters of each other." (Q 17:88)

I, a sympathetic reader, hope to gain access to the excellence and profundity of the Qur'an, I seek evidence of the divine presence Muslims claim emanates from the reading of the book. Notice I said *reading* of the book. There is one aspect of the Qur'an unavailable in this study. *Qur'an* means "recitation," and a Muslim's primary relationship to the book is through chanting its contents or listening to its words chanted in Arabic. All I can do here is access that aspect of the Qur'an that one can reach through reading. The Qur'an, like the Bible, consists of many different types of literature, such as laws, prayers, ritual instruction, and apocalyptic visions. However,

---

1. Citations from the Qur'an will be presented between parentheses like this: (Q 72:1), which refers to the first verse of the seventy-second sura (chapter).

because I encounter the Qur'an as a relatively new visitor, I begin with narrative. It is an easy place to start because everyone relates to a story.

In what follows, I analyze nine stories from the Qur'an. Although some of these Qur'anic tales involve biblical characters (Moses, Solomon, and the Queen of Sheba), those I have chosen scarcely overlap with the Jewish or Christian Scriptures. However, in many ways these stories bring to mind biblical texts, ones that address similar themes and concerns to those found in the Qur'an. Bringing the Qur'an and Bible together in this way enriches understanding of both. John Kaltner observes, "Revisiting a familiar Bible story with the theme and message of its Qur'an parallel in mind can allow us to notice elements of it that have previously gone unrecognized."[2] This remains true even though my work does not examine Qur'anic parallels to biblical texts, as Kaltner does.

My training is in the Hebrew Bible. I here examine what for me is an alien text, a strange text, and a whole interpretive tradition that had been unfamiliar to me. Why have I strayed so far from my chosen field? At least in part, it was because of the Muslim claim that the sublimity and uniqueness of the Qur'an will be obvious in any serious examination. This drew me. I am curious about the attraction to this book and about its veneration by over a billion people.

I chose the nine Qur'anic passages because they were compelling narratives. I looked for stories with vivid characterization and drama. Also, I looked for passages skirting the edge of orthodoxy. I search out Qur'anic texts that appear to represent the earliest stages of Islamic formation. When the community began fashioning its identity, it was at a time when many pre-Islamic practices and beliefs were being examined and reconsidered by the new community. These passages, then, inhabit the borderland between the Islamic community and the surrounding culture. As I approached each of these stories in turn, certain common themes emerged, and this became the structure of my study.

Now a word about my choice of biblical texts. I did not have any Bible passages in mind when I began to analyze these Qur'anic narratives. None of the Qur'anic texts I have chosen has a biblical parallel, except for mention of the queen of Sheba (Chapter 6). Rather, as my knowledge of these suras grew, they brought to mind particular parts of the Bible that were similar, or which might illumine certain obscurities in the Qur'anic story. I found many surprising similarities as well as revealing differences between the Bible and my chosen passages. Overall, I found that both scriptures asked similar questions and faced comparable issues. Most notably, both the

---

2. Kaltner, *Ishmael Instructs Isaac*, 23.

Qur'an and the Bible advocate for exclusive worship of a singular God. The Qur'anic passages I have chosen, and the corresponding biblical texts both make their case as to which parts of the surrounding culture to embrace and which parts to reject in the light of that exclusive worship.

This introduction is not the place to survey the field of qur'anic scholarship. I will, however, briefly situate myself within that vast and creative field.[3] I divide Qur'anic interpretation into these categories, although I realize my divisions grossly oversimplify:

1. Pious interpretations—Islamic commentaries on the Qur'an, called *tafsīr*, make certain assumptions about the text. They take every single word of the Qur'an as God's speech, unmediated by human influence. Therefore, the Qur'an must be true in all it affirms. As a result, these interpreters harmonize disparate elements within the Qur'an so that they say the same thing and so they support Islamic orthodox belief. Early Islamic interpretation made reference to the Prophet's actions and teachings, things not included in the Qur'an.[4] For most subsequent Muslim exegetes, some part of this early post-Qur'anic tradition becomes determinative to later interpretation. Early Muslim interpreters comment on the necessity of these traditions:

   > It is not possible to know the interpretation of a given verse without knowing its history and the causes of its revelation.[5]

   > Exploring the cause of revelation is a firm way to understand the meaning of the Qur'an.[6]

2. Orientalist interpretations—*Orientalist* is a term made famous by Palestinian literary critic Edward Said (1935–2003). Said took the word *orientalist* from art criticism and used it to describe Western scholars who wrote about the Middle East or North Africa and who regard their subject as quaint and primitive. Western Qur'anic scholars making Orientalist interpretations conclude that the Qur'an is derivative, either from Christianity or Judaism or both. They claim that the Qur'an was unoriginal and uncreative.

---

3. Donner, "Reflections" provides a very good survey.

4. Throughout this book I often refer to Muhammad as "the Prophet" (with a capital *P*). When I refer to other prophets, I will use a lowercase *p*.

5. ʿAlī b. Aḥmad al-Waḥḥidi (d. 1075), quoted in Ikhwan, "Interpreting the Qur'an," 216.

6. Ibn Taymiyyah (d. 1328), quoted in Ikhwan, "Interpreting the Qur'an," 216.

3. Contemporary, late twentieth-century and twenty-first-century interpretations—In 2015 I presented an earlier version of Chapter 6 in Yogyakarta, Indonesia, at the State Islamic University, as part of the annual meeting of the International Qur'anic Studies Association (IQSA). It has been my privilege to be present at the birth of this new society, founded in 2012, a community of scholars, Muslim and non-Muslim, global in scope. Having attended and participated in their annual meetings,[7] I have noted the following trends. Most of their research is in the these areas:

- A concern for history, in which the Qur'an is mined as source material to reconstruct seventh-century Arabia and the conditions that contributed to the birth and early years of Islam.

- History of transmission—analyzing how various Islamic communities, ancient and modern, read and understood Qur'anic texts.

- Philological studies—examining the meaning or semantic field of a particular Arabic word or phrase used in the Qur'an and surrounding texts. I include here also discussions of Qur'an translations into English and other languages.

- Thematic studies—what the Qur'an says about a particular topic, such as God, the afterlife, eschatology, and so forth.

- Close reading of Qur'anic texts—I would include myself in this group.

In my work I do not say anything global about the Qur'an or about Islam. I limit the scope of my study to a small sampling of narrative texts. If you picture the Qur'an as a vast mountain (it is!), I am only taking a few teaspoons of matter from the mountain, or perhaps a teacup of water from one of its swift-running streams.

Some of my fellow literary critics, those who engage in close reading of individual suras, often succumb to a harmonizing impulse. When they see a "rough spot" in their passage, a tension or lack of coherence, they find reasons to maintain that if the passage were properly understood, the contradiction or ambiguity would melt away. I contend that the most dynamic parts of these ancient scriptures are located in the spaces between pieces of a text that do not easily fit together. Therefore, my analyses often work *against* harmony. The disruptions and dissonances in the text are the places where meaning is produced. The passages in the Qur'an that I have chosen are those where these lines of tension, these ruptures, are closest to the surface. Rather than being flaws, these fault lines are the sources of the Qur'an's

7. I presented earlier versions of three chapters of this book at IQSA conferences.

power. Thus, each section of this book introduces an unresolved problem the Qur'an must address.

The first section of the book explores the challenge of *polytheism*. Both religions, the Islamic and the Israelite, emerged out of a polytheistic environment[8] and to varying degrees defined themselves distinct from and against that context. From the Qur'an I chose three narratives that examine how Muslims regard those who believed in and worshiped multiple gods. Chapter 1 covers two connected suras (chapters), incantations that protect against malevolent spiritual forces. These forces much resemble the gods and goddesses of surrounding culture. Chapter 2 considers three goddesses who are called "the daughters of God." Their continued presence in seventh-century Arabia constitutes a challenge to Islamic monotheism. Chapter 3 concerns the jinn, a supernatural race with a long history of interacting with humans on the Arabian Peninsula. Although the Qur'an rejects the very existence of goddesses (Chapter 2), the Jinn Sura does not question the reality of these supernatural beings.

The second section of the book examines an issue that every monotheistic faith must deal with: *the problem of evil,* or theodicy. If one believes in a single deity, does that deity then bear the responsibility for all the suffering in the world? Chapter 4 considers divine punishment and its proportionality to the offense. Chapters 5 and 6 through different narratives, consider whether to blame God for human suffering, and if not, why not? These two suras each present a unique figure that serves as proxy for the interrogation of deity. The suras, by exploring the behavior of these unique figures, indirectly reflect upon God's actions. In the Cave Sura (Chapter 5), a figure named in later tradition the Green Man (*'al-Khidr*) stands for God. He appears to Moses in a sacred place and schools him regarding divine behavior. In Chapter 6, King Solomon himself is God-like when he threatens a community of ants. This narrative device (proxy figures standing for God) provides a less dangerous way for Muslims to consider God's liabilities and other transgressive possibilities when addressing the problem of evil. These stories question divine justice only indirectly.

The final section of the book isolates three texts under the heading of *revelation*. Chapter 7 considers how the Qur'an, though a fresh revelation, uses older stories to convey its message. Chapter 8 examines a sura in which two revelatory moments jump-start the career of the Prophet. Finally, Chapter 9 examines what effect the behavior and judgments of the Prophet have on the message.

---

8. See Penchansky, "Polytheism."

In this book, I primarily focus on the Qur'anic narratives I have assembled. Certain connections or similarities exist between these Qur'anic narratives and portions of the Hebrew Bible. In some cases, I only briefly mention a biblical text. In other chapters, consideration about the Bible constitutes up to half of the chapter. In Chapter 2 for instance, I spend equal time with the Star Sura and Proverbs 8. In each chapter, after the chapter title, I list the relevant biblical passages under a subheading, labeled Texts in Comparison.

These chapters trace how biblical communities dealt with similar issues to those in the Qur'anic stories. The Qur'an and the Hebrew Bible share many strategies as they address these three issues, monotheism, theodicy, and revelation. This is not surprising because they raise questions that are intrinsic to revelatory monotheism, that is, a monotheism whose followers regard their sacred text as heaven-sent. Both the Bible and the Qur'an come from the same rough geographic and cultural milieu, although many centuries apart. Additionally, there is ample evidence that the Arabian people in the seventh century had knowledge of many biblical stories in some form. There are of course significant differences in the way the Bible and the Qur'an approach these issues I have listed, and I explore those differences as well. Differences and tensions between the two provide another rich source of meaning.

Although this book focuses on the actual narratives in the Qur'an itself, I will often refer to post-Qur'anic literature, including the early biographies of the Prophet, Qur'anic commentaries (called *tafsīr*), and "occasions of revelation" (*'asbāb al-Nazūl*), stories that emerge in the early Islamic community that tell what happened to inspire each revelation. These sources tend to be determinative for pious interpretations. Although sometimes these occasions of revelation and other ancient sources might represent actual historical circumstances when the Prophet received the messages, more commonly they reveal how the first few generations of Muslims understood the Qur'an in the centuries after the time of Muhammad. Qur'anic scholar Patricia Crone (1945–2015) said this:

> There cannot, of course, be any doubt that in the long run the
> tradition will prove indispensable for an understanding of the
> Quran, both because it preserves early information and because
> it embodies a millennium and a half of scholarship by men of
> great learning and high intelligence on whose shoulders it is
> good to stand.[9]

These post-Qur'anic writings reveal how early readers understood the Qur'an and the strategies they used to understand difficult and confusing texts.

9. Crone, "The Religion of the Qur'anic Pagans," 152.

I frequently resort to a "master narrative" of early Islamic history to explicate a sura. The Qur'an is made up of disparate genres with many themes and stories repeated multiple times in different suras. Very soon after the time of the Prophet, the community of interpreters began to piece together a master narrative, a single coherent story. They were able to fit together the disparate suras and parts of suras like pieces of a puzzle. This master narrative features the following elements that may or may not correspond to the actual history of the formation of the Qur'an.

> The story begins in the city of Mecca, where the beleaguered community of Muslims was persecuted by the ruling tribe, the Quraysh. Muhammad was himself a member of this tribe. Leading members of the Quraysh opposed Muhammad and the fledgling Islamic religion for two reasons. First, they objected to Muhammad's teaching of monotheism (tawḥid) on principle. Second, they opposed Muhammad's criticism of their idol worship because pilgrimages to the shrine of the Ka'ba were a major source of income for the Qurayshi leaders. By opposing the gods housed in the Ka'ba, Muhammad was damaging their bottom line. At some point, the persecution against the small group of Muslims became so intense that Muhammad had to move the entire community from Mecca to Medina.

I locate many of the Qur'anic narratives I examine within this master narrative. Specifically, subsequent Islamic interpretation sees many of these suras as products of the time of persecution, reflecting the dire situation of the suffering community in Mecca. This becomes a helpful way to understand the suras, seeing them as response to this persecution.

Frequently in these chapters I examine breaks in the text—places where key information is missing or is contradictory or in tension with other parts of the passage. It is a principle of Islamic interpretation (and biblical interpretation, and interpretation in general) that the larger context (in this case other parts of the Qur'an) determines the interpretation of a specific text. That is certainly true to an extent. However, all too often this search for a larger context turns into a desire to harmonize an elusive text, making it fit better with the whole. Early Islamic interpreters force any passage that is an outlier to agree with dominant beliefs and conform to their sense of coherence in the Qur'an. This harmonizing impulse does violence to the Qur'an because it marginalizes troublesome texts and fails to listen to their manifold voices. It is far better to examine these ruptures, explore their contours and textures, because these are the places in the text that produce meaning. As Leonard Cohen sang:

There's a crack in everything. That's how the light gets in.

I am full of gratitude to Hend Al-Mansour, my wife, my best friend, and my Arabic teacher. She has been my partner throughout in discussing these texts. There would be no book without her.

شكراً زوجتي الحبيبة هند . . . أحبك

Part I

The Problem of Polytheism

The monotheistic faiths took root and grew in polytheistic soil. Ancient Israel began in a community that worshiped multiple gods. There is ample archaeological evidence that throughout their history at least some of the Israelites continued the practice of modified polytheism. The Bible contains significant traces that attest to this polytheistic and idol worship. For instance, the sons of God in Genesis and in the book of Job (the *bene ha'eloīm*) are a council of divine beings who advise Yahweh.[1] These beings, though not called gods, fulfill the same role as lesser gods in surrounding cultures. The Israelite prophets condemned the worship of Baal and Asherah, two Canaanite deities. They were outraged because these practices and beliefs continued widespread in their communities. We find additional traces of polytheism in Pss 58 and 82. They portray Yahweh, the God of Israel, as member of a vast pantheon ruled by the father-god who was named El. The Greek text of Deuteronomy tells a similar story:

> When the Most High [*'el-'elyōn*] apportioned the nations,
> when he divided humankind,

---

1. See Chapter 3 for a fuller discussion of this biblical passage.

> he fixed the boundaries of the peoples
>> according to the number of the angels;
> the LORD's [Yahweh's] own portion was his people,
>> Jacob his allotted share. (Deut 32:8–9)

The Hebrew text makes no sense when it writes, "according to the number of the *sons of Israel*," and seems an attempt by a later scribe to cover up an embarrassing text. What is meant by "angel" (*angelōn*) in the Greek translation of the Hebrew Bible, and what is the likely Hebrew phrase that underlies this word? The "angels" here were members of the heavenly council, and the consensus is that "angels" represents the Hebrew words *benai 'el* meaning "sons of El," or *benai 'elohīm*, meaning "sons of *'elohīm*" (translated God or gods). The great god El assigns to subsidiary gods the realms he wants them to rule. Yahweh, one of these subsidiary gods, is given charge over the Israelites. This verse in Deuteronomy assumes that many gods exist.

One of the reasons for these polytheistic traces is that there are inherent problems that arise when one maintains a strict monotheism. There are many instances of slippage, where some aspects of polytheism or its trappings maintain a presence within the monotheistic faith, so that it is no longer monotheism in the strictest sense. By the strictest sense I mean a God without other divine, supernatural beings present and without other causes in the universe.

The Qur'an has less tolerance for polytheistic traces than does the Hebrew Bible. Therefore, in order to locate these traces, it is helpful to examine the polemic stories that are written in the Qur'an *against* the existence and worship of other gods. Why rail against something unless it exists as a problem? In "Daughters of Deity" (Chapter 2), I examine this antipolytheism polemic. I find traces of polytheism in the depiction of supernatural beings other than God found in the portrayal of the demonic (Chapter 1) and the jinn (Chapter 3). Because of these irruptions of polytheistic sensibilities, certain texts in the Bible and the Qur'an represent strategies that map out and model ways to deal with the intrusion of "alien," polytheistic influence. These are the strategies:

1. One might claim that these other divine figures do not exist. This is how the Star Sura addresses belief in the "Daughters of God" (Chapter 2).

2. One might claim that spiritual personalities other than God exist, but they are demonic (Chapter 1).

3. One might claim that these other divine figures are servants of the one true God, such as angels.[2] This strategy belongs in the third section of my book, "Prophecy and Revelation," because divine communication is its chief concern.

4. One might claim that the other divine figures have been vanquished, have cowered, and have been made to submit. This is the strategy of the Jinn Sura (Chapter 3).

The early parts of the Qur'an came to the Prophet while he lived in Mecca, a cosmopolitan society whose inhabitants worshiped many gods. One might say that this polytheistic environment provides the backdrop to many of the Meccan suras.[3] The images of their gods resided in the Ka'ba, a cubical shrine located in the city. Whether one begins Israelite monotheism with Abraham, Moses, Elijah, or Ezra, the surrounding communities living adjacent to the Israelites, Judaeans, and Jews, were polytheists. The boundary between the people of the Israelite God and the polytheistic groups was porous. Because both these religious movements (Islam and Yahwism) came out of polytheistic milieus, they both had to decide what to do about the ancient gods and the practices associated with them. One might have suspected that the Qur'an and the Bible would categorically reject all the trappings that remained of their polytheistic past. However, that is not the case. The Muslims called the past beliefs and times of their Arabic ancestors j'ahlīyah, meaning the time of ignorance. In a similar way, Israelite texts describe the surrounding polytheistic cultures disparagingly as "the uncircumcised." When David confronted the giant Goliath, he proclaimed:

> Who is this uncircumcised Philistine to defy the armies of the living God? (1 Sam 17:26)

Both the Bible and the Qur'an express a strong aversion to the stink of polytheism and the trapping of idol worship. However, the new religions did assume or take over some of the beliefs and trappings of older polytheistic beliefs and practices. In most cases, authors conceal the polytheistic origins of these beliefs and practices, suppressing and denying their origin. In order to justify the continuation of these religious observances, they link them to revered figures from the past.

In this way the Muslims retained the Hajj pilgrimage and the circumambulation of the Ka'ba, even though they existed as religious rituals from before the time of Muhammad. Now Muslims associate these practices

2. I address angels in Chapter 8.

3. Islamic tradition divides the Qur'an into suras received in Mecca and suras that came to the Prophet while he ruled in Medina.

with the Patriarch Abraham and his son Ishmael. According to the Qur'an, Abraham and his son built the Ka'ba. In the ancient Near East, the ritual slaughter of animals was common practice before Yahweh became ruling deity. The Hebrew Bible presents sacrifice as a divine command, and so it continued as a key element in Israelite worship. Neither early Islam nor early Yahwism rejected all the ancient gods and goddesses. Instead, they redesignated some as angels and others evil spirits, and in the Qur'an they included the jinn. Others of these ancient gods and goddesses, subsumed by God, became a particular quality or characteristic of the Great Deity. Muslims celebrate the ninety-nine names of God as a sign of deity's manifold aspects, but the names just as well reflect the qualities of ancient gods and goddesses that now become the qualities of Allah, a word that literally means *the* God.

A central teaching of Islam, known as *tawhid*, means "oneness." *Tawhid* insists there is no one like the one God. For this reason, Muslims will not call God Father, because no human role can shed light on God's nature. They find the idea of God having a son objectionable because God does not have children as humans and animals do.

> He has not begotten and was not begotten. (Q 112:3)

The most extreme form of *tawhid* would not allow the existence of other supernatural beings such as angels or devils. Islam does not go that far, but lays down a strict line between the uncreated God and every other being. The three Qur'anic passages (suras 113 and 114 together come from a single point of view) map out the way the Qur'an addresses the possibility of other supernatural beings and what might be their relationship to the one God. The suras in the following chapters do not challenge *tawhid*, but they do problematize it.

These first three chapters explore how the early followers struggled to separate out what was pure and acceptable to their new movement, and what God required them to reject.

Surat-al-Falaq Q 113

In the Name of God, the Merciful, the Compassionate.

Say: "I take refuge with the Lord of the daybreak,

from the evil of what He has created

and from the evil of darkness when it looms,

and from the evil of the women who blow on knots,

and from the evil of an envier when he envies."

Surat-al-Nas Q 114

In the Name of God, the Merciful, the Compassionate.

Say: "I take refuge with the Lord of the people,

the King of the people, the God of the people,

from the evil of the whispering one, the slinking one,

who whispers in the hearts of the people,

of the jinn and the people."

I

Surat-al-Falaq (The Daybreak) and Surat-al-Nas (The People)

Q 113 and Q 114— The "Taking Refuge" Suras

Texts in Comparison: Genesis 1; Job; Isaiah 45:7; Matthew 6:13; 1 Thessalonians 2:14–16

THE TWO SURAS

The two last suras (chapters) in the Qur'an, suras 113 and 114, are called Surat-al-Falaq (translated "the Sura of the Dawn," or "the Sura of the Daybreak,") and Surat-al-Nas (translated "the Sura [concerning] humans.") Muslims call these suras sisters because of their proximity to each other, and their similarity. After the conventional introduction, the bismillah,[1] they both begin:

> Say, "I seek refuge . . ."

---

1. Every sura but one begins the same way, with the bismillah. The entire phrase may be translated, "In the Name of God the Merciful, the Compassionate."

For this reason, they are called the two seeking-refuge suras, the *mu'wadhatain*. They are structurally similar and theologically controversial. Cook notes,

> This *sura* and the following final *sura* have been controversial
> in Islam; some early copies of the Qur'an did not include them
> as part of the authoritative text. The language and grammatical style of the *suras* are difficult, and can be explained only by
> twisting the rules of Arabic grammar.[2]

They are controversial because they portray a world filled with malevolent supernatural forces opposed to humans.

They are anomalous when compared to the rest of the Qur'an. Their unique tone engendered controversy in the early centuries of Islam. They were attacked, reinterpreted, and vehemently defended by different segments of the community. They do, however, occupy an important place in Islamic piety. Parents recite them to calm crying babies, and they are used to turn aside curses.[3]

These suras are among the shortest in the Qur'an. The suras in the Qur'an are arranged roughly in order of length, and these two are the last. They have two distinct introductions. First, there is the general inscription, "In the Name of God, the Merciful and Compassionate," the bismillah. The bismillah is formulaic, that is, a set piece meant to begin the recitation of the sura, and it provides a kind of authoritative stamp of inclusion. When this phrase appears in front of a sura, that makes it a legitimate part of the Qur'an.

In addition, these two suras have a second introduction that sets them apart from all but a few suras: the command to "say." God as speaker commands the hearer to "say" something. The audience (the one to whom the command "say" is addressed) is either Muhammad, the community, or both. But if we bracket out these two introductory phrases—the bismillah and "say"—then the speaker is no longer God but one who presents to God a petition. The speaker wants God to provide refuge. The petitioner regards God as the audience of his appeal. The first line might be rendered,

I seek refuge from [you, O] Lord of the Dawn. (Q 113:1; my trans.)

(The "you" is not in the Arabic but is implied.) The line can be read two ways. It may address a current, desperate situation. In this reading, the line is not a general declaration of faith, which would say, "This is the God I turn to whenever I need refuge." Alternatively, this opening line might be read

---

2. Cook, "The Prophet Muhammad," 325.

3 L'Hopital, "Prayer Formulas," 233, says these suras are "frequently employed."

as a general declaration of faith to the community, a declaration of loyalty to a particular God or to a particular manifestation of God—although this alternate reading is more speculative.

What follows the command to "say" is what the hearer must recite. After the command to say, the speaker declares, "I seek refuge from . . ." Fatani observes that the word translated "I seek refuge" has two objects. The first object is the protector, the goal, the Lord of the Dawn.[4] The second object is the source of the danger. In this verse, the petitioner flees *from* the danger, *to* the place of safety. The threat and the petitioner are actively moving. The threat moves towards the petitioner. The petitioner moves away from the danger into the protective arms of the Lord of the Dawn, the refuge-giver.

In Surat al-Falaq, the petitioner requests to hide in a safe place provided by *rabbi-al-falaq*, "The Lord of the Dawn." Surat-al-Nas also has this movement, from danger to the Lord. The petitioner seeks refuge from *rabbi nas,*[5] translated "Lord of the people." This, the second of the *mu'wadhatain* (the second seeking-refuge sura), then offers three different realms that God controls, all linked to the word *nas* (people):[6] **Lord** of the people (*rabbi nas* Q 114:1), **King** of the people (*malaki nas* Q 114:2), **God** of the people, (*'ilehi nas* Q 114:3). Fatani observes:

> This five-line chapter, or sura, is a semi-formulaic prayer, an address to God . . . invoking His protection and aid from a number of "evil" sources. It has a simple and repetitive semantic structure; "I seek-refuge with X from the evil of Y_1 and from the evil of Y_2 and from the evil of Y_3 and from the evil of Y_4."[7]

After "Say . . ." and "I seek refuge in . . ." and "the Lord of. . ," these suras identify the sources of the danger from which the petitioner seeks refuge.

CONTROVERSY REGARDING INCLUSION OF THESE SURAS

Early Muslims struggled over the inclusion of these suras in the Qur'an. One of he Prophet's earliest disciples considered one of the Companions of the Prophet questioned their legitimacy. Juynboll reports: "the Companion

---

4. Fatani, "The Lexical Transfer," 66.

5. This word is more commonly translated "man" or "mankind."

6. "Lord" is the equivalent to the Hebrew *'adonay*. "The term *rabb* thus appears in the earliest parts of the Qur'an as the generic term for 'a god,' or 'the god' of a certain person or people" (Welch, "Allah and Other Supernatural Beings," 734).

7. Fatani, "The Lexical Transfer," 67–68.

'Abdallah b. Mas'ud(d. 32/653) purportedly opposed their being included in the *Muṣḥaf*[8] (that is, the Islamic canon) but whether or not that is histori- cally accurate could not be ascertained."[9]

There is also inferential evidence that suggests serious controversy re- garding the inclusion of these two suras. Many early commentators argued strenuously *for* their inclusion in the Qur'an, thus indicating that a group existed questioning their legitimacy. Further, one finds accounts that began to circulate reporting that the Prophet himself advocated the inclusion of these suras. Again, this points to the existence of a faction opposing their inclusion. In the Hadith it says,

> I asked the Prophet about them. He said, These two suras have
> been recited to me and I have recited them (Therefore they are
> present in the Qur'an). So we say as Allah's Messenger said.[10]

Accounts began to circulate of how the Prophet recited these suras in his own devotional practice. The authenticity of these suras had been questioned by some, and as a result subsequently defended by others by associating them with the Prophet.

Early Muslims questioned the authenticity of these suras. For one thing, they do not express common Islamic concerns. Second, they lack many of the elements common to other parts of the Qur'an: for instance, they do not argue for monotheism, and they make no reference to biblical stories or characters. Finally, they do not reflect the situation of first- or second-generation Muslims. That is, they have strange names for God, unusual in the Qur'an.[11] Supernatural beings other than God take center stage in these suras. These suras provide a magical script to ward off malign supernatural beings. Such rituals would have been part of pre-Islamic prac- tice, and thus we may consider parts of these suras pre-Islamic, taken over and legitimated by their association with the Prophet. The Qur'an uneasily owns these suras, so there has to be special instruction given about how to handle them. That is why in that instruction, God commands the reader or reciter of, or listener to, the sura to "say this"—that is, specific things (and not to say specific other things).

---

8. *Muṣḥaf* means "bound volume," roughly equivalent to what Christians mean by "canon," that is, an approved list of fixed books.

9. Juynboll, "Hadith and the Qur'an," 393.

10. Bukhārī, *Sahih Al-Bukhari*, vol. 6, book 60, hadith 500.

11. This verse comes close: "(He is) the splitter of the dawn, and has made the night for rest, and the sun and moon for reckoning. That is the decree of the Mighty, the Knowing" (Q 6:96).

CLOSE READING OF THE TWO SURAS

Sura 113: Surat-al-Falaq

After the dual introduction, both suras begun "I seek refuge . . ." This verb necessarily has two indirect objects, (1) what the petitioner is running *toward*, and (2) what the petitioner is *fleeing*. In the case of sura 113, the petitioner flees toward *rabbi al-falaq*, "the Lord of the Dawn."

"The Lord of the Dawn" is an unusual designation for God. In what way is God "Lord of the Dawn," and why would God be identified in that way in this sura? What is there about the dawn that makes it particularly important that God rule over it? Is the dawn the enemy that the Lord overcomes? Or is the dawn so beautiful that God must be the source of such beauty, and thus he is the Lord of the dawn?

At base, the word *falaq* means "splitting." There is a much more common word for dawn, *fajr*, which is used elsewhere in the Qur'an meaning "dawn," and it is the Muslim's word for the sunrise prayer. "Splitting" comes to mean "dawn" presumably because dawn is the dividing line (the splitting point) between the night and the day. But others have suggested that *falaq* here means "creation," because creation is a kind of splitting apart of things. Seeds grow when their casing splits apart; light splits apart from darkness, dry land from the sea; heaven and earth are divided.

God separated the light from the darkness. (Gen 1:4)

The dawn can be a good thing, the coming of enlightenment, the passage from darkness into the light. Two lines later, the speaker seeks from the Lord of the Dawn protection against three dangers. First, he seeks protection against lightless spaces.

I seek refuge from the evil of encroaching darkness. (Q 113:3; my trans.)

But *falaq* can also be a bad thing, a threatening thing. Dawn is a liminal place, a place of danger because neither one thing (day) nor the other (night). The Lord of the Dawn might be someone who rules that realm to the ill of humankind, as the next verse ("from the evil of what He has created") suggests. However, I agree with Fatani, who says, "The immediate context ("I seek refuge with the Lord of X") does not clearly point to a certain interpretation because there are no contextual cues."[12]

The second verse introduces the second danger. It says:

12. Fatani, "The Lexical Transfer," 71.

[I seek refuge] . . . from the evil which he has created.

For the most part, the Qur'an's approach to the problem of evil draws from the same playbook as Christianity. When they address the question of God's complicity with evil, both Christians and Muslims offer similar defenses. They blame evil and suffering on human free will and the temptations of Satan. God will restore balance to the universe at the great judgement but is not responsible for how things have gone wrong. This verse in Surat-al-Falaq diverges from the traditional explanations and borders on blasphemy, because it blames God for evil:

I take refuge . . . from the evil of what He has created. (Q 113:1–2)

There are many pious explanations for the transgressive nature of this verse.[13]

Some have suggested that the verse refers to the evil that is now in the created world, without asserting that God is responsible. However, this is not grammatically possible unless you emend the text. Yusif Ali translates this verse without a subject:

. . . from the mischief of created things.

By his wishful thinking, Ali seeks a way to divert attention from an embarrassing text.

Other pious readings suggest that God created the world good but it became corrupted. It is that corruption that is here referenced, and not something that God created. However, the plain meaning, although theologically incorrect, would read the verse like this:

. . . from the evil that he [that is, the Lord of the Dawn] created.
(my trans.)

Traditional monotheistic approaches to the interpretation of this verse deflect responsibility for evil away from God, blaming the devil and humans. Although these approaches recognize that God created the world and is responsible for everything in it, they reject the possibility that God is in any way responsible for evil.

The book of Isaiah makes a similar assertion to the sura's transgressive verse. God declares in Isaiah:

I form light and create darkness,
    I make weal and create woe;
    I the LORD do all these things. (Isa 45:7)

13. See Chapters 5 and 6 for a discussion of God as the source of evil.

In the book of Job, the protagonist accuses deity of unfairly attacking him, violating justice, and being the source of his pain and suffering.[14] Even in the New Testament, Jesus instructs his disciples to plead with God that God not lead the believer into temptation (Matt 6:13). This prayer explicitly states that God *might* lead believers into temptation if they do not offer the prayer, or if the prayer proves ineffective. Monotheism has always faced the tension between on the one hand attributing to God all movement and existence in the universe, but on the other hand declaring God wholly good. These passages in the Bible and the Qur'an suggest that some within these traditions saw God as ultimately responsible for the evil in the world. They saw God's responsibility for evil as a necessary component of the belief that God is the source of everything. Others within both traditions found reasons to exonerate God.

This passage in the Qur'an places the responsibilities for the evil clearly and explicitly upon the shoulders of the Lord of the Dawn. And by placing this sura in the Qur'an as indicated by the addition of the introductory formula, bismillah, the author identifies the Lord of the Dawn as the one God. Therefore, this suggests a portrait of God that differs from the dominant Qur'anic conception. This one, the Lord of the Dawn, creates evil and threatens humans.

In this sura, God creates evil, and the petitioner seeks the source of refuge in God the refuge-giver, against or from God the source of dangerous evil. One Islamic interpreter exclaimed,

> I take refuge with thee from thyself.[15]

The next verse of sura 113 speaks a new evil to be feared, "encroaching darkness." The verb "encroaching" has the sense of flowing over something. The word for darkness, *gh'asiq*, is related to the Hebrew word for darkness (*ḥošek*), used in the book of Genesis in the first creation story. It says that before God's first creative word, when all was chaos,

> darkness (*ḥošek*) covered the face of the deep. (Gen 1:2)

In this verse of the Qur'an, "encroaching darkness" picks up this same light-darkness theme, but only if we interpret *falaq* as "dawn."

The Lord of the Dawn cannot be fully trusted. Although the believer finds refuge in the Lord of the Dawn, it is a mixed blessing because the Lord of the Dawn also creates evil. It is not necessary for the Lord of the Dawn to be the only God in order to be the creator of evil. One might see the tension

14. See Chapter 6 for a fuller discussion of the book of Job.

15. Padwick, *Muslim Devotions*, 83–93.

of this verse between the notion that God is responsible for everything, including evil, and the notion that God is wholly good and not responsible for evil—the tension between a God who is a refuge for the believer and a God who is also evil. A God both good and evil is a monotheistic concept—a God who encompasses both extremes and is therefore beyond all dualities.

The third danger from which the petitioner seeks refuge is from

> the women who blow on knots. (Q 113:4)

Tying knots and blowing on them was a common means for casting spells among the Arabian and North African tribes. Relevant to understanding this verse are the ancient stories that emerged about Muhammad in the second and third generations of Islam.

Accompanying most suras there circulates "the occasion for the revelation" (*'asbāb al-Nazūl])*—that is, they give an account of the circumstances in the Islamic community at the time when Muhammad received a particular sura from God. These stories also provide a guideline for readers as to how the suras should be interpreted. Cook notes regarding this accompanying narrative that "this short sura [113] . . . is usually interpreted in the light of this single story,"[16] by which he means the story of Muhammad's "occasions of revelation" taken together. The stories of these occasions (see below) need not be historical (although they are framed that way) but were rather produced by the first Islamic community for purposes of teaching and establishing the official narrative and accepted lines of interpretation for the individual sura. These stories function similarly to the way the midrash functions in Jewish tradition.

The stories that surround the *mu'wadhatain* make their connection though this single verse about women blowing on knots (Q 113:4). They seek to explain how these suras were given to Muhammad in order to ward off the curses that the knots inflicted upon the Prophet. Two categories of stories have been connected with the origin of the *mu'wadhatain*. In the first, the sura describes how the Prophet uses these suras in personal devotional rituals and to turn away curses lodged against him. The following is found in the Hadith, the stories and teachings of the Prophet:

> 'Ā'ishah [Muhammad's wife] narrated: "Whenever the Prophet went to bed every night, he used to cup his hands together and blow over them after reciting . . . Surat al-Falaq . . . and Surat al-Nas . . ., and then rub his hands over whatever parts of his body

16. Cook, "The Prophet Muhammad," 325.

he was able to rub, starting with his head, face and front of his body. He used to do that three times."[17]

The Prophet is also reported to have similarly recited the Throne Verse (Q 2:255) and the two refuge-taking chapters (Q 113, 114), and blown into his hands and wiped his face and body so as to physically spread the healing benefit of the suras over his person for protection.[18]

In Haditha Sahih the Prophet (peace be upon him), every time he went to bed, he would put his palms together, blow on them, and then recite the Taking-Refuge Suras. Then he strokes whatever parts of his body he can reach with his hands. He starts with his head and his face, and then the front of his body. He does this three times.[19]

The second category of story tells of Muhammad's bewitchment. The women, by blowing on the knots, cast an evil spell upon the Prophet. One cannot determine whether the bewitchment story or the devotion story came first, which depended upon the other, or if they existed independently. In a plausible scenario, one could imagine that people would be uncomfortable with the idea of the Prophet succumbing to bewitchment. The devotion story arose then as an alternative, providing a superior reason for Muslims to accept the authority of these suras. Many within the Islamic community could not conceive that the Prophet of God could be subjected to evil forces. "Thus, for a magician to manifest the ability to deny the Prophet this power is evidence of great power, and an issue with which later commentators felt very uncomfortable. The Prophet does not come off looking very impressive here."[20]

The devotion-story genre instructs readers to use these suras to ward off evil in a dangerous world, as did the Prophet. The second story—the bewitchment story—problematizes that message a bit. In the bewitchment story a Jewish man, ʿĀṣim Ibn Lubaid, casts a spell upon Muhammad. This is during the time when Muhammad is struggling to establish an Islamic community in Medina. That Muhammad's tormenter is a Jew is significant. Throughout history, Jews have been castigated for not joining this or that new religious movement. When Muslims gained power in Arabia, they persecuted the Jews in a similar manner to the way European Christians persecuted Jews who lived among them. Cook notes: "We find also a strong connection between

---

17. *Sahih*, viii, 110, no. 4372, quoted in Gade, "Recitation of the Qur'an," 369.

18. An-Nabbi, *Medicine of the Prophet*, 148–49, 180

19. Al-Thaʿalibi, *Tafsīr Al-Thaʾalibi*, 4:453 (my trans.).

20. Cook, "The Prophet Muhammad," 239.

Jews, women, curses, and sexuality which does not appear by chance. Women are said to be the majority of the inhabitants of hell because of their excessive cursing. The curse is also uniquely attached to the Jews as well."[21]

As Muhammad began to establish control over Medina, he came into conflict with many powerful groups. Among them were Jewish tribes and Jewish merchants, whom Muhammad forbade to trade with Mecca, a major commercial hub. The city of Mecca at this time opposed Muhammad. The Ibn Lubaid story (as distinct from any information gleaned from sura 113 itself) reflects the conflict between Muhammad and the Jewish tribes. It shapes the interpretation of the sura. For many, the sura no longer serves as a warding off of evil but rather as a polemic against the Jews because they competed with Muhammad's community both commercially and politically. In this climate of competition, it is common for those in power to demonize their opponents. This explains the association of the Jews with Muhammad's bewitchment, and why later interpreters cast them as the "enviers" in the last line:

> [I take refuge . . .] from the evil of an envier when he envies.
> (Q 113:5)

However, the sura itself does not connect the "women who blow on knots" or the "enviers" to the Jews.

In the most common form of the story, Ibn Lubaid's daughters curse Muhammad, tying eleven knots in a cord and casting spells by blowing on each knot successively. Then Ibn Lubaid throws the cord in a well. At that point, something afflicts to the Prophet. In some accounts, he becomes (what we would call) clinically depressed. Cook recounts how many ancient sources describe Muhammad as "in a catatonic state."[22] One commentator suggests that "some of the limbs of the Prophet were out of his control for a time."[23] Or alternatively, he suffers a physical sickness. A strong and persistent tradition has suggested that Muhammad becomes incapable of sex with his wives as the result of the spell. Cook quotes an ancient (ninth-century) Shia commentator who said, "The Prophet went for three [days] without eating, drinking, hearing or seeing anything or going to women [for sexual

---

21. Cook, "The Prophet Muhammad," 343. "The idea of Jewish magic is also deeply rooted in the Muslim tradition. . . Ka'b al-a'ār bears witness to this need to defend oneself from the magic of the Jews. As he says, 'If it were not for the words [of magic] that I say at sundown and sunrise, the Jews would have transformed me into a barking dog or a neighing donkey. I take refuge in the protecting words of God, which neither righteous nor evil [people] can pass'" (Cook, "The Prophet Muhammad," 344).

22. Cook, "The Prophet Muhammad," 323.

23. Cook, "The Prophet Muhammad," 333.

intercourse]. Then Gabriel came down to him and brought down with him the *mu'wadhatain*."[24]

Commentator Al-Wahidi (d. 1075) puts it this way: "The Messenger of God sickened and his hair fell out. He would think that he went into his women, when he did not go into them."[25] In any case, neither his Companions nor his wives could revive him.

Muhammad receives a vision in the night of two angels, one at his foot and one at his head. They inform the Prophet that his condition is the result of bewitchment. They tell Muhammad where to retrieve the knotted cord, and they give him these two suras to turn back the bewitchment. The Prophet's Companions retrieve the cord, and as they loosen each successive knot, Muhammad became that much improved. By the last knot, he is fully restored.

The bewitchment story conflates two apparently separate versions—one where the discovery and undoing of the knots brings deliverance, and another where the recitation of the suras brings deliverance. There is no place that says to undo knots *and* recite the suras.

In some versions the knots are untied by the Companions of Muhammad. In others the knots are burned and so the spell is broken. In some Muhammad gets the cord. In others his Companions get it. The results of the curse are different in different versions of the story. And in some versions, Ibn Lubaid is the culprit and not his daughters.

This story troubled many Muslims. They considered it inconceivable that the Prophet could be subject to bewitchment. "It was the story of Labaid al-Yahudi [Labaid the Jew] and his bewitching of the Prophet Muhammad which made them [the early commentators] the most uncomfortable."[26] Cook goes on to cite Al-Alusi (d. 1853), who "relates all (or virtually all) versions, and then decries the story as impossible and condemns it in the strongest terms available."[27]

Others claimed that the spell only *seemed* to work on Muhammad, but in fact the knots were powerless to affect him. Q 113:4 (and its backstory) became a point of controversy within the early interpretive community.

In the final line in Surat al-Falaq, the petitioner seeks refuge

From the evil of an envier when he envies. (Q 113:5)

This verse is anticlimactic. The sura moves from the Lord of the Dawn, who creates evil rising up as barriers and snares for humans (Q 113:2), to

24. Cook, "The Prophet Muhammad," 327.
25. Cited in Cook, "The Prophet Muhammad," 331.
26. Cook, "The Prophet Muhammad," 324.
27. Cook, "The Prophet Muhammad," 324.

the darkness that expands like the spreading of oil (Q 113:3), to cruel witch-
es casting spells on the Prophet (Q 113:4), to evil enviers (Q 113:5). Some
commentators recognize the problem because they try to demonstrate (un-
successfully, and a bit shrilly) that envy is the root of all the other evils, and
so it appropriately belongs at the climax of sura 113. Another suggestion
is that the envy of the enviers refer to Jews who envied Muhammad's fresh
revelation and his political success. However, this connection between envy
and the Jews only occurs to later interpreters. That is, someone subsequently
asked, who were these enviers and why are they dangerous?—and gave the
answers that the Jewish tribes were envious of the Prophet, and their people
were powerful, malign sorcerers. Kahn gives further evidence in the Qur'an
connecting envy with "the Jews":

> In Q 113:5, the worshipper seeks divine protection from "the
> envy of the envier." In Q 2:19, the "people of the Book," [Jews
> and Christians] out of envy seek to turn believers into unbe-
> lievers . . . This is a theme especially developed in the life story
> of Muhammad in his relations to the Jews of Medina, whose
> refusal to convert is portrayed as resulting from envy.[28]

There is a bare hint of this suspicion about the Jews in the Qur'an itself, although much less than one finds in later Islamic tradition. It says in
another sura:

> Do you not see those who have been given a portion of the
> Book? . . . [that is, the Jewish tribes.] They believe in al-Jibt and
> al-Taghut. [Probably names of gods.] . . . (Q 4:51)
> Or are they jealous of the people for what God has given them of
> his favor? Yet we gave the house of Abraham the Book and the
> wisdom, and we gave them a great kingdom. (Q 4:54)

Muhammad is deeply disappointed that the Jews do not embrace his
teaching and become Muslims. In a similar way, in the New Testament, Paul
rails against his Jewish contemporaries who do not embrace Christianity:

> For you suffered the same things from your own compatriots
> as they did from the Jews, who killed both the Lord Jesus and
> the prophets, and drove us out; they displease God and oppose
> everyone . . . Thus they have constantly been filling up the mea-
> sure of their sins; but God's wrath has overtaken them at last.
> (1 Thess 2:14–16)

---

28. Kahn, 224–25.

This predilection to castigate Jews, which one finds in both Qur'an and the New Testament, reflects the disappointment of both Christians and Muslims that the Jewish community did not immediately recognize and embrace the new revelation and the new prophet. The polemic reveals far more about the accuser than the accused.

Sura 114 Surat-al-Nas

In the second of the *mu'wadhatain* suras, the petitioner seeks refuge at the court of a thrice-designated deity.

> Say, I take refuge with the Lord of the People, the King of the people, the God of the people. (Q 114:1–3)

Three names, three alternative identities, are written: *Rabbi Nas* [Lord of people], *Malaki Nas* [King of people] and *Ilehi Nas* [God of people]. *Nas* means "people," humanity in general. These are unusual names, not elsewhere used to describe deity.

The petitioner seeks refuge from the danger of the whisperer:

> from the evil of the whispering one, the slinking one. (Q 114:4)

Most commentators identify the "whisperer" as Satan. He is described as a whisperer because he whispers evil inclinations into human hearts. There are two possible lines of interpretation regarding this. One might understand the withdrawal of the whisperer as a sneaky, hiding action; alternatively, the whisperer withdraws in fear when the *nas* recite this sura.

THE TWO USES OF *NAS*

The whisperer whispers in human hearts (*fisidū al-nas*). The sura then elaborates by adding: "from the jinn and the humans" ("human" is that same word, *nas*). That ends the sura and is the last verse of the Qur'an.

The two different uses of *nas* disrupt the word's meaning. In the first use, the *nas* is the victim. The whisperer whispers into the heart of the *nas*, and it is the *nas* that prays this prayer for refuge. In the second usage, the *nas* is one of the sources for the whispering:

> who whispers in the hearts of the people [*nas*], of the jinn and the people [*nas*]. (Q 114:5–6)

Jinn whisper and the *nas* whisper. The jinn[29] have long been associated with Satan, and they were widely regarded as an invisible source of temptation.

> (Remember) when we said to the angels, "prostrate yourself before Adam," and they prostrated themselves except Iblis. He was one of the jinn, and acted wickedly (against) his Lord. (Q 18:50)

The Islamic commentators suggest that the second *nas* refers either to evil people who seek to tempt the righteous, or else to internal evil inclinations.

However, there is a too-loose grammatical connection between, "[the one] who whispers into the heart of the *nas*" and "from the jinn and the *nas*." Many in their translations and interpretations add a phrase to make sense of the last three words. They add something like "*the whispers which come* from the jinn and the nas." "*The whispers which come*" is not in the text but is added to make sense of the last phrase.

Consider the two phrases together without the addition:

> Who whispers in the hearts of *nas*
> From jinn and *nas*. (my trans.)

Something is wrong here. There is no need for another subject who whispers. One already exists—the whisperer, Satan. Now instead the whispering comes from two previously unmentioned sources, jinn and *nas*. One expects the jinn to whisper. The jinn in Arabic belief (in popular English "genie") are a parallel race with supernatural powers and a tendency toward evil.[30] But the other victimizer is identified as *nas*—the very *nas* over which the refuge-giving God is Lord; the very *nas* into whose heart the whisperer is whispering. Perhaps these are different *nas*. The whispering *nas* are evil ones who afflict the good *nas*.

It appears that something has occurred to weaken the structure of the verse. Such a textual disruption results when something has been removed, changed, or added inelegantly. In some cases an offending passage has been excised or neutralized, but the smoothness of the text suffers. If some words were censored, one must ask, why was not the whole excised to relieve the tension and stress that they caused? Perhaps the phrases were too widely known and accepted by either the community or its potential members, and so had to remain, leaving traces in the present text. There is not enough left to suggest what might be missing. Even with this awkwardness, sura 114

29. See Chapter 3, which is about the Jinn Sura.
30. Some jinn upon hearing the Qur'an became Muslims. I discuss this in Chapter 3.

paints a picture of supernatural warfare where evil beings from multiple metaphysical realms are shooting whispers, darkness, and curses at each other—a nightmarish scenario.

These two suras are transgressive for the following reasons. They ascribe evil to God. They serve an apotropaic function; that is, they turn away curses. The stories that accompany the early interpretations portray the Prophet using these suras for that purpose. These suras employ unusual names for God, and they regard God as a shelter from a universe filled with dangerous spirits. These invocations probably existed in some form as prayers before Muhammad's time. For the Islamic community, they were considered revelatory when they became part of the instructions from God. When God commanded "say," that granted sanction to use them against curses. The addition of the bismillah made them canonical. They became instructions from God to aid believers in avoiding curses and threats from supernatural forces.

Parts of these suras must have come from pre-Islamic times.[31] Like other religious communities at their beginnings, the early Islamic community raided its own culture (in this case, seventh-century Arabia) to provide content for their religion.

It should not be seen as strange or even disrespectful that parts of some suras were added to the Qur'an from pre-Islamic sources. Suras 113 and 114 give divine approval for their own inclusion with the single word, "Say," which makes them part of Muhammad's revelation. Why should there not be a protective incantation taken from ancient Arabic lore included in the Qur'an? And this kind of assimilation by Islam of older Islamic prayers is not a one-way street. The objects of veneration and incantation exert a shaping function to the religions that employ them. By including in the Qur'an a description of the universe as a crowded with supernatural entities other than God, these suras troubled the strict monotheism of Islam (tawhid). This troubling is not a flaw, but rather enriches the Qur'an. The presence of powerful supernatural forces competing with God and thus thwarting the Prophet, made these incantations necessary.

In these suras, a community works out its relation to the other spirit-beings believed in by the wider society. The prayers of the mu'wadhatain reflect unusual pre-Islamic ideas, which Islam had to process and assimilate. Welch correctly maintains:

> The central Muslim doctrine of the "oneness" [tawhid] of God
> unfolded gradually in the Qur'an . . . the gradual polarization of

---

31. See Chapter 2 for another example where a sura, in this case the Star Sura, uses a pre-Islamic prayer.

other supernatural powers, beginning with an acceptance of the
ancient Arabian world view involving other deities and the jinn,
and ending with essentially Judeo-Christian view of One God,
His angels, and Satan.[32]

Every monotheistic religion must destabilize its monotheism in some
way, because religion requires some multiplicity in its construal of God to
account for a plural and ambiguous universe. It is a manifestation of Freud's
idea, "the return of the repressed." In Freud's theory, when one represses a
difficult and painful experience, in this case a polytheistic universe, it inevi-
tably comes back in some other form, usually disguised. "What is forgotten
is not extinguished but only repressed; its memory-traces are present in all
their freshness, but isolated by 'anticathexes.' . . . they are unconscious—inaccessible to consciousness."[33]

These two suras, the *mu'wadhatain,* provide the necessary alternative
to the tendency of philosophical monotheism to become rigid. This explains
both these suras' controversy and their persistence. In these suras, the "repressed," polytheism, comes back in this picture of a world crowded with
dangerous supernatural entities.

In summary, these suras developed in four stages: first, a prayer for
protection is widely known in the Arab community. Second, this prayer
becomes part of a liturgical practice. Third, participation in the liturgical
curse removal is enjoined by the imperative "say." Then fourth, this liturgy
becomes incorporated in the official collection of suras, as indicated by the
beginning bismillah. The first two steps, the prayer and the liturgical practice, might have occurred before Muhammad's time.

The Qur'an drinks deeply from the religious milieu of seventh-century
Arabia. We usually think of the Qur'an as reacting against its culture. After
all, Muslims refer to pre-Islamic Arabia as "the time of ignorance" (*j'ahlīyah*).
And yet many things pre-Islamic moved unhindered into the Muslim community. As in the Hebrew Bible, the path to monotheism came not only
though a rejection of the other gods, but also through their assimilation. The
one God absorbed their qualities and attributes.[34] So as one examines the
Lord of the Dawn, the Lord, King, and God, of the *Nas,* there is not only the
one God but perhaps also traces of other gods subsumed by that God. This
adaptation was not one-sided; rather, these ancient representations of deity
contribute something to the understanding of God in the Qur'an.

32. Welch, "Allah and Other Supernatural Beings," 733.

33. Freud, *Moses and Monotheism,* 94.

34. For my discussion on these ideas in the Bible see Penchansky, *Twilight of the
Gods.*

Surat-al-Najm Q 53:19–25:

Have you seen al-Lat, and al-Uzza, and Manat, the third, the other? Do you have male (offspring) while He has female? Then that (would be) an unfair division! They are only names which you have named, you and your fathers. God has not sent down any authority for it. They only follow conjecture and whatever they themselves desire—when certainly guidance has come to them from their Lord. Or will a person have whatever he longs for? To God (belongs) the last and the first.

2

Surat-al-Najm (The Star Sura)
Q 53:19–25—Daughters of Deity

Texts in comparison: 1 Kings 13; Proverbs 8; Sirach 23;
Wisdom of Solomon 7; Baruch 3

The "taking refuge" suras in the previous chapter depict a supernatural world where terrifying forces surround and threaten the faithful. In this chapter, the "daughters" of the chapter title represent a different category of supernatural beings. They too challenge the strict monotheism of the Qur'an. Goddesses like these appear in the Qur'an and the Bible. Both books refer to these figures not only as goddesses but as "God's daughters." As daughters, they share God's divinity in some way. They are important, powerful, but are "softer" than God, and serve as an intermediary, a mediatrix between the Father-deity and his worshipers. These "daughters" have access to God in ways humans do not. As much as these daughters of God threaten monotheism, the traditions in the Bible and the Qur'an soundly reject any talk of goddesses. However, in what follows here, we note that this rejection has qualifications.

The book of Proverbs introduces the divine daughter Ḥokmah. *Ḥokmah* is the Hebrew word for "wisdom." The feminine ending (*ah*) suggested to the early Israelite sages that wisdom is a goddess, the source and embodiment of wisdom. In Proverbs 8 she speaks about herself and how Yahweh gave birth to her. She says,

24

When there were no depths, I was brought forth. (Prov 8:24)

That is the biblical divine daughter. The Qur'an mentions divine daughters in Sura 53, the Star Sura, Surat-al-Najm. It says:

Have you seen al-Lāt, and al-'Uzzā, and Manāt, the third, the other? (Q 53:19, 20)

The sura offers these three pre-Islamic, pan-Arabic goddesses for the reader's consideration.[1] "Have you considered them?" it says. I here focus on these two appearances of God's daughters—once in the Star Sura, the other in Proverbs. I also trace Ḥokmah, the Hebrew divine daughter, when she appears in other biblical texts. I consider the varied strategies by which Islamic and Israelite communities dealt with the belief in goddesses, a devotion which predates their monotheism.

THE BIRTH OF ḤOKMAH

The Israelite goddess Ḥokmah is "brought forth" (ḥolatîi).[2] Ḥolatî evokes the writhing motions of a woman in childbirth. The other words used to describe her beginnings, qannî:

The LORD created me at the beginning of his work,
the first of his acts of long ago. (Prov 8:22)

. . . and nasakti:

Ages ago I was set up,
at the first, before the beginning of the earth (Prov 8:23).

These two words may also be construed as alluding to birth.[3] Lang carries the birth imagery further than many. He says,

---

1. An oddly defensive claim by Maududi understands the verse to say, "Have you ever considered rationally whether they could have even the slightest role in the affairs of the Godhead of the earth and heavens?" (Maududi, *Meaning*, 249). "Have you considered," from the root *r ' '* to see, meaning in this form, "to form an opinion, to consider." Some translators (for theological reasons?) retain "see." "Have you considered" [these three goddesses] implies that they would be worthy of serious consideration, even if ultimately one rejects the premise. "See" is a more neutral rendering.

2. Brown et al., *A Hebrew and English Lexicon*, 297, from the word *ḥûl* meaning "to writhe." These other verses use similar language referring to childbirth: Isa 26:17; 45:10; 51:2; Job 39:1; Ps 90:2.

3. See my discussion in Penchansky, *Twilight of the Gods*, chapter 6; and Penchansky, *Understanding Hebrew Wisdom*, chapter 2.

While the creation of the material world can be referred to in terms of craftsmanship and building activities[,] . . . Wisdom's creation must be spoken of in personal terms: Wisdom was "begotten" [his translation of *qanna*], "fashioned" [*nasaq*] (as in the womb), and eventually "born." Gods are not created as the world is created; they are begotten and born, not made. There is a qualitative difference between gods and the realm of the created.[4]

Lang continues:

She is not the product of the artisan's skill, nor has she been conquered in battle to be made part of the ordered world. Rather, she has been *born* or brought forth by birth. Wisdom says of herself, "I was born (*holati*)," an expression used to refer to human birth.[5]

When there were no depths I was *brought forth*. (Prov 8:24)

The word is used a second time in v. 25:

. . . before the hills, I was brought forth. (Prov 8:25)

Yahweh is Ḥokmah's divine parent. He is both father and mother. Something similar occurs in other ancient sources. Adam gives birth to Eve, who emerges out of his male body. In Greek mythology Zeus gives birth to Athena out of his head. Lang observes,

Within religious history there are several gods without mothers, and Wisdom may belong to these . . . Similarly, the Egyptian god Thoth . . . sprang from the head of Seth. Such paradoxical phenomena are labeled "male pregnancy" and "male birth," ideas not entirely foreign to the Bible.[6]

Some scholars compare Ḥokmah to the Canaanite divinity Asherah. However, Asherah is a mother goddess while Ḥokmah is not. Yahweh himself is the birth parent.

Claudia Camp observes, "The process of Yahweh's conception, bearing and birth of Wisdom is here depicted without reservation."[7] Yahweh gives birth to wisdom, and then she, as a small child, sits in rapt attention as Yahweh, her father, creates the universe.

---

4. Lang, *Wisdom and the Book of Proverbs*, 77

5. Lang, *Wisdom and the Book of Proverbs*, 63.

6. Lang, *Wisdom and the Book of Proverbs*, 64–65.

7. Camp, *Wisdom and the Feminine*, 82, 84.

When he marked out the foundations of the earth,
  then I was beside him, like an *amôn* [little child];
and I was daily his delight,
  playing before him always. (Prov 8:29, 30 NRSV, altered)

The NRSV and many others translate the bracketed term "master worker." The word *amôn* occurs only here in the Hebrew Bible. Through close cognates interpreters have offered two definitions: "master worker" and "little child, nursling." When it says that Ḥokmah was "playing before him," that suggests either children's play or sexual play.[8] In this context, "child's play" is the better choice because she plays "before him," not "with him." Ḥokmah builds nothing, but only plays, giving Yahweh delight. Lang observes, "To play before the head of household in this part of the world was to be part of the family. It speaks of deep intimacy."[9]

Following her birth, Ḥokmah compares herself to the elemental forces present at the birth of the universe.

Ages ago I was set up,
  at the first, before the beginning of the earth.
When there were no depths I was brought forth,
  when there were no springs abounding with water.
Before the mountains had been shaped,
  before the hills, I was brought forth—
when he had not yet made earth and fields,
  or the world's first bits of soil.
When he established the heavens, I was there,
  when he drew a circle on the face of the deep,
when he made firm the skies above,
  when he established the fountains of the deep,
when he assigned to the sea its limit,
  so that the waters might not transgress his command,
when he marked out the foundations of the earth. (Prov 8:23–29)

Notice the verbs. The deep, the primal waters of creation, are *inscribed*, the mountains are *shaped*, the heavens are *established*, and the fountains *abound* in water. These others function as *things* for Ḥokmah to admire. What a contrast with these two verbs that describe Ḥokmah's activity. She

8. According to Brown, Driver, Briggs, (965), the definitions of the word are "laugh" or "play." "Play" is further broken down to mean (a) to make sport; (b) jest; (c) play an instrument, singing, dancing, merry making; (d) children's sport; (e) mock. A cognate word is used to describe Isaac's fondling of Rebekah (Gen 26:8). In Gen 26:8 the word is used, translated "Isaac *fondles* his wife."

9. Lang, *Wisdom and the Book of Proverbs*, 78.

"plays," and she "delights." Yahweh delights in her, and she in turn delights in humanity. One finds a similar use of the word "delight" in Jeremiah:

> Is Ephraim my dear son?
> Is he the child I *delight* in? (Jer 31:20)

Ḥokmah bridges in this word "delight" the human and the divine realms, in that Yahweh delights in her and she in turn delights in humanity. Yahweh created the universe to give delight to his young child.

Subsequent to the writing of Proverbs,[10] the atmosphere in Israel became increasingly hostile to goddesses. Surprisingly however, the figure of Ḥokmah persists in the writing of successive generations of Israelite sages. In Ben Sira (dated no later than 180 BCE), Ḥokmah finds her home in Jerusalem:

> Among all these I sought a resting-place;
> in whose territory should I abide?
> Then the Creator of all things gave me a command,
> and my Creator chose the place for my tent.
> He said, "Make your dwelling in Jacob,
> and in Israel receive your inheritance."
> Before the ages, in the beginning, he created me,
> and for all the ages I shall not cease to be.
> In the holy tent I ministered before him,
> and so I was established in Zion.
> Thus in the beloved city he gave me a resting-place,
> and in Jerusalem was my domain. (Sir 24:7–11)

Finally, Sirach reveals Ḥokmah's true identity. She is *Tōrah*:

> All this [the previous self-revelations of Ḥokmah/Sophia]
> is the book of the covenant of the Most High God,
> the law [Hebrew: *Tōrah*[11]] that Moses commanded.
> (Sir 24:23)

In Sirach, the writer quotes Ḥokmah:

> I came from the mouth of the Most High,
> and covered the earth like a mist. (Sir 24:3)

---

10. The first ten chapters of Proverbs are regarded as some of the last verses to be added to the book, dated perhaps to the fifth century BCE.

11. The Hebrew of chapter 24 is lost. The Greek word used here, *nomos*, is the Greek translation of the Hebrew word *tōrah*.

Coming out of deity's mouth, Ḥokmah becomes the Word of God. This comparison was not lost on the first Christian community, who borrowed descriptions of Ḥokmah to describe the Christ. For instance,

> He is the image of the invisible God, the firstborn of all creation; for in him all things in heaven and on earth were created, things visible and invisible, whether thrones or dominions or rulers or powers—all things have been created through him and for him. (Col 1:15–16)

Note these similarities:

Colossians 1	Proverbs 8
"Firstborn of all creation"	"created me at the beginning."
"in him all things created"	"When he established the heavens, I was there,"[12]
"created through him. . . for him"	"daily his delight" (Prov 8:30)

In the Wisdom of Solomon (from around the first century BCE into the first century CE), Ḥokmah (her Greek name is Sophia) represents the creative force of deity, what theologians call hypostatization, a personified *aspect* of God:

> For she is a breath of the power of God,
>   and a pure emanation of the glory of the Almighty. . .
> For she is a reflection of eternal light,
>   a spotless mirror of the working of God,
>   and an image of his goodness. (Wis 7:25–26)

And from the book of Baruch (whose dating is uncertain),

> Who has gone up into heaven, and taken her,
>   and brought her down from the clouds?
> Who has gone over the sea, and found her,
>   and will buy her for pure gold?
> No one knows the way to her,
>   or is concerned about the path to her. (Bar 3:29–31)

> She is the book of the commandments of God,
>   the law that endures for ever. (Bar 4:1)

---

12. Later tradition makes Ḥokmah the source of creation.

LAT, UZZA, AND MANAT

In the Qur'an, the issue appears explicit and clear—one must choose between the goddesses whom the people worshiped in the time of ignorance and the one true God; Nevertheless, one finds subtle undercurrents and traces of an older position that acknowledged the goddesses, or at least considered the possibility of their existence. The two aforementioned lines in the Star Sura bring these undercurrents to the forefront:

> Have you considered[13] Lat and Uzza, and Manat, the third, the other? (Q 53:19, 20; my trans.)

I will first survey where these three goddesses appear in pre-Islamic archaeological artifacts and inscriptions; second, I look into in the Star Sura and its larger Qur'anic context; finally, I consider the Star Sura in the context of early Islamic tradition, including an account of the so-called Satanic Verses that stand behind the Star Sura.

PRE-ISLAMIC ARCHAEOLOGICAL EVIDENCE

The worship of these three goddesses, Lat, Uzzah, and Manat, was widespread geographically from Sinai in the west, to Syria in the north, spreading to all of Arabia. People dedicated temples to them and carved statues to represent them. They left their stamp on many personal names mentioned in ancient texts and inscriptions. We lack, unfortunately, any religious texts that narrate their stories and mythologies. Greek historian Herodotus mentions Lat, and she has been compared to and identified with both Aphrodite and Athena. Earliest references to Lat date to the fifth century BCE. According to Islamic tradition, Arabs worshiped the three goddesses in Mecca and neighboring towns. Muhammad's tribe, the Quraysh, identified particularly with Uzza. Here is Bowersock's overview:

> These three names appear significantly in epigraphical evidence from early Arabian and Nabatean archaeological sites. They represented the names of goddesses worshipped in that region through large tracts of its history. However, there is no real consensus on what these goddesses might represent. Uzza is regarded by some as the Arabian Aphrodite. From etymology of names, Manat (death), Uzza (strength), and Lat (goddess: Al-Lat: "the goddess," the feminine version of Al-lah, "the god").

13. Droge, trans., *The Qur'an*, is nearly alone in translating this word as "see." Its root is from *r'h* ("see"), but in this form it means to consider something as an option.

Perhaps at some point Lat's actual name was hidden, replaced by this generic name. They are major female deities in the region.[14]

Therefore, when the Star Sura enjoined its audience to *consider* the three goddesses, the audience already knew them. Their widespread worship is one of the reasons Muslims describe the time before the coming of the Prophet as "the time of ignorance, the *j 'ahlīyah.*

THE STAR SURA AND
THE LARGER QUR'ANIC CONTEXT

After the above quoted lines, a new voice breaks in and responds incredulously. The literal translation is this:

> Is it to you the male and to him [presumably God] the female?
> (Q 53:21; my trans.)

I understand the verse to mean the following:

> How can you covet male children for yourselves while you ascribe to God these daughters, Lat, Uzza, and Manat?[15]

I consider some aspects of this argument below, but for now please note that the Star Sura presents Lat, Uzza, and Manat as putatively God's daughters.

To recapitulate, ancient Israel developed toward a single, all-consuming absolute monarch as its image of deity. That would leave little room for a figure such as Ḥokmah, and yet she persisted. Islam condemns *shirk,* the comparing of God with any created thing. That would prohibit any Islamic consideration of goddesses, and yet here the reader is enjoined at least to consider the possibility of their existence. Whence comes this ambiguity?

Ḥokmah does indeed persist, but in such a way that she does not challenge the official monotheistic position. For Israelites and subsequently in Jewish thought she became a symbol of the abstract principle wisdom, and a way of speaking about God but not an actual goddess with an existence and identity separate from God. By contrast, following the introduction of the three goddesses, the Star Sura emphatically rejects their existence. The sura gives many reasons why it is ridiculous to accept these goddesses. First because they are female. The author asks,

---

14. Bowersock, "An Arabian Trinity," 20.

15. This is my paraphrase/translation. Droge translates it, "Do you have male [offspring] while he has female?"

Is it the male for you, and for him [God] the female?
[and then observes] That is indeed an unfair division.
(Q 53:21, 22, literal rendering based on Droge)

The Star Sura assumes that daughters are less desirable than sons. Therefore, it is absurd to think that God, the superior one, would deign to have daughters.

The sura opposes belief in the goddesses because they are

names you have named. (Q 53:23)

The sura claims that the names Lat, Uzza, and Manat have no substance that underlies them. They are merely names with no corresponding existence. They have no reality. The third reason to reject the goddesses is that God did not authorize the three goddesses to intercede on behalf of their worshipers. In fact, God rarely allows anyone to intercede on behalf of believers:

How many an angel there is in the heavens whose intercession
is of no use at all, until God gives permission to whomever He
pleases and approves? (Q 53:26)

The fourth reason for no goddesses is that those who do not believe in the hereafter are the only ones who give female names to angels. I should note that in various suras the label on the three goddesses shifts from "daughters of God" to "female angels":

Surely those who do not believe in the Hereafter indeed name
the angels with the names of females.(Q 53:27)

From the perspective of the Qur'an, every right-thinking person believes in the hereafter because the necessity of its existence is so patently obvious. Therefore, the Star Sura argues, the same people who want the three goddesses to intercede for them are then those who are foolish enough to deny the afterlife. They are not worth listening to. That is sufficient reason to reject their claims; and finally the fifth reason to reject the three goddesses is that God has already provided help, so there is no need to ask for help from the goddesses:

certainly guidance has come to them from their Lord.
(Q 53:23)

Other places in the Qur'an also speak of these divine daughters, without mentioning their names, Lat, Uzza, and Manat. Similarities of language and concern suggest that whether they refer to them as God's daughters or female angels, these other passages refer to the same Lat, Uzza, and Manat.

> Or has he taken (for Himself) daughters from what He creates, and singled you out with sons? . . . Yet they have made the angels . . . females. (Q 43:15–19)

> Has your Lord distinguished you with sons and taken (for Himself) females from the angels? Surely you speak a dreadful word! (Q 17:40)

> And they assign daughters to God . . . and to themselves (they assign) what they desire. When one of them is given news of a female (child), his face turns dark and he chokes back his disappointment. (Q 16:56–58)

> Does your Lord have daughters while they have sons? Or did We create the angels female while they were witnesses? (Q 37:149–50)

In this early stage, the Islamic community included those who worshiped female angels. The implications of Muhammad's radical teaching were slowly sifting through the community, which at that point consisted of an admixture of Arabic cultural and religious practices and beliefs, as well as original ideas and new ways of speaking. Each practice and belief had to be considered separately. It appears that at some point at Islam's beginning, the community seriously considered the three goddesses and their inclusion in Islamic piety. This possibility and its ultimate rejection is the subject of these verses. Through this sura and many others, very quickly Muslim authorities cleared out the Arabic pantheon. Henceforth the universe would be populated by angels, devils, and jinn, but only one God, and absolutely no female angels or deities.

In these aforementioned verses, it is unclear whether the sura accedes to the belief that daughters are inferior to sons. It is at least possible that rather than disparaging women, it exposes the hypocrisy of those who prefer male children and yet worship female gods. In any case, the rejection of goddess worship and divine daughters is unequivocal. However, the Qur'an would not have railed against such beliefs unless they had been widespread and popular within their community. What would compel people to seek out these three goddesses? What kind of help did people hope to derive from Lat, Uzza, and Manat? We get a clue in the Star Sura. It says,

> How many an angel there is in the heavens whose intercession
> is of no use at all, until God gives permission to whomever He
> pleases and approves. (Q 53:26)

This verse addresses people who looked to these three goddesses for
intercession, that is, as a means by which humans bring their needs to God.
Even the angels (presumably the male ones) fail as intercessors most of the
time. The verse asks, How can you suggest that these goddesses can provide
you with effective representation with God when even the angels in heaven
rarely prevail in these efforts? Other suras also address the rarity of success-
ful angelic intercession. For example,

> Who is the one who will intercede with Him, except by His per-
> mission? (Q 2:255)

> Or have they taken intercessors instead of God? Say: . . .
> Intercession (belongs) to God altogether. (Q 39:43–44)

Seeking these three goddesses for help was absurd at the outset, for
all these reasons. After the Qur'an became a fixed book, Islamic tradition
expanded the narrative.

EARLY ISLAMIC TRADITION

Two centuries after the death of the Prophet, Ibn al-Kalbi wrote *The Book
of Idols,* a compendium of pre-Islamic gods, goddesses, and religious practices. In it, he describes a chant heard in Mecca while the pre-Islamic pagan
Arabic worshipers circled the Ka'bah:

> I swear by Lat and Uzza,
> And Manat, the third the other.
> Indeed they are the exalted goddesses [*gh'araniqatu*]
> Whose intercession is to be sought.[16]

The first two lines are nearly identical to vv. 19 and 20 of the Star Sura.
"Have you considered" is replaced by the oath formula, indicated by the
prefix, the letter *waw*, translated "I swear by. . ." One sees a similar form in
v. 1 of the Star Sura:

> [I swear by] the star when it falls! (Q 53:1)[17]

---

16. Al-Kalbi, *The Book of Idols*, 17.

17. See Chapter 8 for a discussion of the first part of the Star Sura.

The Book of Idols portrays the pre-Islamic Meccans seeking these three goddesses for intercession. Al-Kalbi reports that the Quraysh (rulers of Mecca) called them "the daughters of God." Regarding the word translated "exalted goddesses" (*gh'aranīqatu*), its basic meaning first refers to certain seabirds, in which case women and goddess are called *gh'aranīqatu* because they in some way resemble or invoke these birds. However, *gh'aranīqatu* conveys nothing to the modern reader and has remained obscure for over a millennium. The word itself does not occur in the Qur'an. One does, however, find the word used in pre-Islamic poetry. Based on the poetry, definitions range from "seabirds" (herons or cranes) to "women" to "goddesses." With the further descriptor "high," the word means either "*high*-flying birds," "*highborn* women," or "*high (flying)* or *exalted* goddesses."

THE SATANIC VERSES

There exists an ancient Islamic narrative that explains why these unusual verses in the Star Sura bear such a remarkable similarity to the prayer to the goddesses in Ibn Kalbi's *Book of Idols*. The narrative explains why the sura might reproduce a part of this older, pre-Islamic chant. The earliest accounts of the story I am about to relate actually predate *The Book of Idols* and appear in many texts from the first two centuries of Islam, distributed widely throughout the region. The story has come to be known as "the Satanic Verses." It is mentioned in almost every interpretation of the sura in the first two centuries of Islam, and it was a standard element in the stories circulated about the Prophet. Opposition to the authenticity of the story did not arise until the tenth century:

> The reports of the Satanic verses [are] incident to the late first and early second centuries [to the seventh and early eighth centuries according to the Gregorian calendar[18]], in other words, to what seems to have been the earliest period of systematic collection and organization of historical memory materials in the Muslim community.[19]

Burton says, "The inflexible monotheism normally attributed to the Prophet's message was not so central to it as is often supposed."[20]

18. Ahmed uses the Hijra calendar, which dates from when Muhammad took his community to Medina and established the first Islamic state.

19. Ahmed, "Satanic Verses," 258.

20. Burton, "Those Are High Flying Cranes," 249.

There were political implications in the use of these two lines as well. See Q 17:73–74 which Maududi translates,

> (O Muhammad), they had all but tempted you away from what We have revealed to you that you may invent something else in Our Name. Had you done so, *they would have taken you as their trusted friend.* Indeed, had We not strengthened you, you might have inclined to them a little, whereupon We would have made you taste double (the chastisement) in the world and double (the chastisement) after death, and then you would have found none to help you against Us.[21]

Droge translates the verse,

> Surely they almost tempted you away from what We inspired you (with), so that you might forge against Us (something) other than it, and then they would indeed have taken you as a friend And had We not made you (stand) firm, you would almost have been disposed toward them a little.

The gist is that the Prophet is tempted by Satan to make up verses and claim them a revelation from God. Muhammad might want to do this in order to endear himself and his community to the ruling Quraysh.[22] Abdullah Saeed has noted in a recent article:

> [Given] the close connection between the Qur'anic text and Hijazi tribal culture[, the culture in the territory that includes Mecca and Medina,] . . . the Prophet Muhammad wanted to teach new ideas about God without discarding certain prevailing ideas.[23]

Combining all the accounts about the Satanic Verses into one eclectic version, we have this:

The Prophet publicly recites the Star Sura for the first time. After vv. 19 and 20, ("Have you considered Lat, and Uzzah, and Manat . . . ?"), he includes the two verses previously mentioned, from the earlier pre-Islamic prayer:

> These are the exalted goddesses [*gharaniqu*] to be sought for intercession.

Muhammad wanted very badly to bring the members of his tribe into the community of Muslims. The Quraysh were drawn to the Prophet, but

---

21. Maududi, *Meaning,* 53 (italics added).

22. See Chapter 9 for another example where the Prophet faces a similar temptation.

23. Saeed, "Reading the Qur'an Contextually," 154

they wanted to continue to bring their petitions to the three goddesses, as they had in the past. The Prophet received a revelation that sanctioned the intercession of these three, called "the daughters of God." Unfortunately, the revelation came from Satan, and not from God. When the Prophet sanctioned the goddesses' intercession by reciting these ancient verses, the Prophet got what he wanted. The Quraysh became believers. By acknowledging the goddesses, the Prophet made it easier for the Quraysh to submit to his teaching:

> The fact of the Prophet's taking words suggested to him by Satan as being Divine Revelation is presented as arising directly from the Prophet's misplaced desire which, in turn, is clearly influenced by the harsh circumstances.[24]

> The Prophet is portrayed by the Quran as being over-concerned to win over Quraysh.[25]

When the Prophet sanctioned their continued worship of the goddesses, the Quraysh declared their willingness to follow Muhammad in Islam. They accepted Islam because the Prophet accepted their goddesses. Now they could also continue to participate in the cult of the three daughters of God. That night, the angel Gabriel came to the Prophet and corrected him. The angel gave him the verses pertaining to the three goddesses (vv. 19–31), and then the whole became the Star Sura as it now exists.

They are only names which you have named. (Q 53:23)

Muhammad came back the next morning and rescinded permission concerning the goddesses. As a result, the Quraysh abandoned him and his religion. Here is one version:

> When he had reached this verse, the devil suggested to Mahomet an expression of thoughts which had long possessed his soul; and put into his mouth words of reconciliation and compromise such as he had been yearning that God might send unto his people, namely: These are exalted Females. And verily their intercession is to be hoped for . . . They make intercession with Him for us.[26]

This was a time when the Quraysh tribe had been mercilessly persecuting the small band of Muslims.

24. Ahmed, "Those Are High Flying Cranes," 263.
25. Ahmed, "Those Are High Flying Cranes," 270.
26. Burton "Those Are High Flying Cranes," 246.

The Prophet concludes the sura with this final call for prostration at the end of the sura,

> Prostrate yourselves before God and serve (Him)! (Q 53:62)

This is how Burton describes the appearance of the angel to the Prophet:

> That evening, the angel Gabriel appeared to the Prophet and said, "What is this that you have done? You have repeated before the people words that I never gave you."[27]

Muhammad immediately and publicly removed the offending verses. When the Quraysh learned of this, they persecuted the Islamic community again.

For the first two hundred years or so after the time of the Prophet, Muslims knew the story of the Satanic Verses and used it as the key by which they understood the Star Sura.

> Thus the satanic verses incident seems to have constituted a standard element in the memory of the early Muslim community about the life of Muhammad.[28]

After a few centuries, many in the Islamic community began to question whether the Prophet would make such a serious error, whether such a breach was worthy of a prophet of God. Regarding the Prophet in Islam, Mohammad Ahmed observes, "Modern scholarship has long recognized that . . . the early Muslims perceived Muhammad as human and fallible, and it was only later . . . that a superhuman image emerged of Muhammad being immune to sin and error."[29]

The story is consistent with *biblical* portrayals of prophets.[30] In the Hebrew Bible many prophets experience such momentary confusion about their prophetic voice. In 1 Kings 13 for instance, God commands the "man of God from Judah" to refrain from eating or drinking while on his prophetic mission to the North. Then the "old prophet from Bethel" gives him a divine command that he should come home with him and enjoy a meal. The man of God believes the old prophet even though his message is fake.

---

27. Burton, "Those Are High Flying Cranes," 247.

28. Burton, "Those Are High Flying Cranes," 250. No Shia of any school accepts the Satanic verses as representing a true and valid story about Muhammad. This is because the Shia see Muhammad incapable of sinning. Even among Sunni commentators, many question the story. Some interpreters argue that the goddesses are unimportant figures in the region, and that is why Muhammad thought it a small concession.

29. Ahmed, "Satanic Verses," 268.

30. See Chapter 9 for further discussion of flawed prophets.

> I also am a prophet as you are, and an angel spoke to me by the
> word of the LORD: "Bring him back with you into your house so
> that he may eat food and drink water." [The narrator breaks in
> to reveal the true situation.] But he [the old prophet of Bethel]
> was deceiving him [the man of God from Judah]. (1 Kgs 13:18)

In another case, the biblical prophet mistakes his own passion for the
voice of God. When King David tells the prophet Nathan about his plans to
build a temple to Yahweh, Nathan, in a burst of enthusiasm and sycophancy
assures David that God approves his plan.

> The king said to the prophet Nathan, "See now, I am living in a
> house of cedar, but the ark of God stays in a tent." Nathan said to
> the king, "Go, do all that you have in mind; for the LORD is with
> you." (2 Sam 7:2, 3)

Nathan was wrong and had to retract his words.

> But that same night the word of the LORD came to Nathan: "Go
> and tell my servant David: Thus says the LORD: "Are you the one
> to build me a house to live in?" (2 Sam 7:4–5)

This story is quite similar to the night visit of Gabriel to correct Muhammad in the Islamic story of the Satanic Verses.

In sacred stories, sometimes these false prophetic messages come from
an evil spirit. In 1 Kings 22 court prophets assure King Ahab that he will win
a strategic battle against Aram. Michaiah ben Imlah, a prophet not in the
king's employ, reports on a vision of heaven in which Yahweh sends a "lying
spirit" into the mouths of the prophets so that they will deceive the king. As
a result, the king's forces go into battle and are defeated. The king, mortally
wounded, bleeds out in his chariot during the Israelite retreat. The king's
prophets have all listened to a lying spirit. That is why they had encouraged
the king, as Michaiah reveals.

> And the LORD said, "Who will entice Ahab, so that he may go
> up and fall at Ramoth-gilead?" Then one said one thing, and
> another said another, until a spirit came forward and stood be-
> fore the LORD, saying, "I will entice him . . . I will go out and be
> a lying spirit in the mouth of all his prophets." (1 Kgs 22:20–22)

The biblical God tolerates these prophetic missteps, and sometimes
even encourages them. However, he hates willful false prophecy uttered to
gain the approval of the powerful. Jeremiah ruthlessly condemns Hananiah
the prophet, because Hananiah prophesies from his own mind, and not
from divine revelation.

And the prophet Jeremiah said to the prophet Hananiah, "Listen, Hananiah, the LORD has not sent you, and you made this people trust in a lie." (Jer 28:15)

Regarding the Prophet in Islam, Ahmed observes:

The Satanic verses reports illustrate three related themes that are present in the early Muslim writings regarding the life of Muhammad: Muhammad's fallibility; the progressive development of Muhammad's understanding of his Prophethood and mission; and Muhammad's struggle, while in Mecca, to hold fast to the divinely ordained purpose of his Prophethood.[31]

This represents an earlier understanding of the Prophet.

When the later Islamic community increasingly distanced itself from the Israelite prophetic tradition, they began to question the Satanic Verses narrative. In their minds, Muhammad could no longer resemble a fallible, complex Hebrew prophet. Rather, later Muslims portrayed the Prophet as perfect and incapable of error. Ahmed notes, "It was hardly possible for the exemplar of the Law to be allowed to err himself."[32]

Most commonly, Islamic scholars stated that the Satanic narrative lacked the proper pedigree—that is, it does not have a chain of witnesses and so did not pass muster among the medieval Islamic scholarly community.

First, the incident contradicted the theological principle of infallibility in the transmission of Divine Revelation, thereby calling into question the integrity of the text of the Qur'an. Second, the 'isn'ads of the reports which narrated the incident were insufficient in Hadith methodology for the narratives to be validated as true.[33]

(The word 'isn'ad refers to the lineage of a particular story about the Prophet. If the lineage could be traced all the way back to one of the Companions of the Prophet, Muhammad's original circle of disciples, it had more authority than one that did not.)

However, the main motivation to reject the Satanic verses appears to be theological. Sayyid Maududi, a conservative, twentieth-century cleric and interpreter, states a common contemporary position: "To accept the

---

31. Ahmed, "Satanic Verses," 268.
32. Ahmed, "Satanic Verses," 368.
33. Ahmed, "Satanic Verses," 3.

report [the Satanic Verses narrative] means there is no strong basis for belief in any of the teachings of Islam."[34]

Burton summarizes this position: "Muhammad's reported conduct on this occasion would have given the lie to the whole of his previous prophetic activity."[35]

Although many contemporary Islamic interpreters regard the Satanic Verses as a threat to Islam, the earlier traditions had no difficulty with the concept of a fallible Prophet. Therein lies the difference between those who do and do not accept the Satanic Verses.

THE DESIRE FOR GODDESSES

However we read these later developments in the interpretation of the sura, there is no question that the Prophet (and the Star Sura) categorically reject the goddesses. In the Hebrew Bible, the Israelite sages developed a different strategy by which to co-opt and reinterpret the figure of Ḥokmah. Like the Muslims, they too needed to address the people's desire to worship feminine deities. The sages made Ḥokmah (Wisdom) a symbol of Torah, or of God's creative power, and not a distinct and separate being. By contrast, the Qur'an rejects as false even the *names* of these goddesses:

> He said, "Abomination and anger from your Lord have fallen upon you. Will you dispute with me about names with you have named, you and your fathers? God has not sent down any authority for it." (Q 7:71. There is a similar verse in Q 12:40)

However, the Qur'an does acknowledge their desirability when it describes the human attraction to these goddesses. First, the Star Sura introduces the Prophet as one who

> does not speak out of desire. (53:3; my trans.)[36]

The sura regards not being subject to desire as an admirable trait. It then observes that the people seek the three goddesses for intercession because such a relationship satisfies *their* desire, using the same word as in v. 3.

> They only follow conjecture and whatever they themselves desire. (Q 53:23)

Finally, the sura asks,

34. Maududi, *Towards Understanding*, 55.
35. Burton, "Those Are High Flying Cranes," 248.
36. The Droge translation is, "nor does he speak on a whim."

Or will a person have whatever he longs for? (Q 53:24)

The expected answer to the question is, No, of course not. Therefore, the obvious conclusion is that one ought not turn to goddesses for intercession even in the presence of a strong desire to do so.

These three goddesses, Lat, Uzza, and Manat, are the same as the angels with female names in v. 23 and the same as the angels attempting to gain audience with God for purpose of intercession in v. 26. The sura rejects these goddesses, of course. However, it recognizes that the wider community *desires* female gods. In this context, the sura presents its Prophet as desireless, free from the desire to call upon these female names for intercession.

Your companion [the Prophet[37]] has not gone astray, nor has he erred, nor does he speak on a whim [desire]. (Q 53:3)

However, the Star Sura, accompanied by the Satanic Verses tradition that envelops it, suggests that at least for a moment, the Prophet himself felt drawn to the goddesses, and had to be corrected and redirected.

The wisdom tradition in Israel dealt with this desire differently. It too had to adapt to a climate that was increasingly intolerant of divine figures distinct from Yahweh. So for them Ḥokmah became a literary conceit, receiving paeans to her virtues at a time when no one any longer took her seriously as a distinct divine figure. The Israelite effort to placate the desire for goddesses rendered her two-dimensional and ideological in the later texts that speak of her.

The earlier Western scholars of the Qur'an claimed that the Satanic Verses narrative would have so troubled the first generation in Islam that these early Muslims could not possibly have made up such a tale. For that reason, they conclude that the story had to be historical.

This is the indubitably authentic story—it is impossible to imagine a Muslim inventing such an inauspicious tale . . . [It] would not merely have given the lie to all his previous claims to be a genuine prophet, but would certainly have finished him for the future.[38]

It is hardly possible to conceive how the tale, if not in some shape or other founded in truth, could ever have been invented.[39]

37. These are other verses that identify the Prophet as "your companion." Q 34:46 and 81:22.

38. Burton, "Those Are High Flying Cranes," 254, 257.

39. Ahmed, "Satanic Verses," 535.

These interpreters claim that because this story undermines basic Islamic notions regarding the Prophet, it would never have endured unless it had actually happened. On the contrary, for the first two centuries of Islam, many Muslims knew the story and it did not trouble them at all. The profusion of sources for the story gives evidence of this, and that there was no pushback against its inclusion in the tradition until two hundred years afterwards. "They [the early Muslims] did not view the incident as inauspicious."[40] Therefore, the oddness of the story neither supports nor excludes its historicity.

Do not mistake what I am saying. No part of the tradition seeks to rehabilitate the Satanic Verses themselves. In every ancient version of the story, the Prophet ultimately rejects the Satanic Verses. In some, the Prophet realizes it by himself, but in most versions the angel Gabriel must correct him. In no version does Muhammad concoct the story to achieve political ends (although it supports his political goals). Nor does he willfully turn over the sura to evil spirits. No version condemns the Prophet. "Muhammad is portrayed as being under pressure, confused, and unaware of the import of his act."[41]

Tabari (839–923) and others suggest that God intended *this* verse in Surat-al-Hajj (sura 22) to comfort the Prophet after he had momentarily listened to Satan, because he feared God's chastisement for his error:

> We have not sent any messenger or any prophet before you, except that, when he began to wish, Satan cast (something) into his wishful thinking.[42] But God cancels what Satan casts, (and) then God clearly composes His verses. (Q 22:52)

According to this narrative, God takes out the Satanic Verses and replaces them with vv. 21–28 of the Star Sura as presently constituted. Thus, the sura rejects the pre-Islamic chant that was later reported by Al Kalbi. The Satanic Verses narrative then highlights the integrity of the Prophet, who does not allow concern for his reputation or authority to prevent him from admitting and correcting his error. The story also speaks of the integrity of the revelation itself, that God would send an angel to make sure that it was right. It portrays the process by which the Prophet, the Quraysh, and the Islamic community tooled out what they would take from their past, and what they would leave behind and reject. The Star Sura itself asks,

40. Ahmed, "Satanic Verses," 535.

41. Ahmed, "Satanic Verses," 264.

42. This "wishful thinking" reflects the Prophet's desire to heal the breech between the Muslims and his tribe.

Have you considered the three goddesses? (Q 53:19; my trans.)

No one in later Islam would ever ask a question in that way, on that topic. Later commentators try to make the question mean, Have you considered how absurd are these goddesses? But the question in its original form is studiously neutral. In its very neutrality the question stands apart from later Islamic orthodoxy. The sura quoted from this part of the ancient polytheistic chant (vv. 19–20) the trace of a strongly held belief now passing away, like a broken monument standing in mute reminder of past glories.

We might imagine that goddesses found it difficult among both the ancient Israelites and the early Muslims during the transition of each group to monotheism. The changes forced these deities to compete in a field increasingly dominated by a single deity. Many gods accepted demotion and became messengers or servants in the divine court. They dropped their customary honorifics and became angelic emissaries, devils, satans, and jinn. On top of that demotion, the goddesses faced the increasingly monotheistic universe that was also very patriarchal and masculine. In Israel, many of the goddesses went underground, accepting worship and petition from secret gatherings consisting mostly of women. However, in Israel, Ḥokmah retained her title through many divine purges by virtue of her importance to the wisdom tradition and the sages. In the Qur'an, goddesses did not fare so well. One bare mention, two verses in the Star Sura, and then the opening shuts forever.

Islam has taken over much from earlier religious practice. It linked those practices to older narratives about righteous monotheists such as Abraham. However, intercession by Lat, Uzza, and Manat became a bridge too far, too big a stretch for the new religion. Nevertheless, for one tiny moment at least, a small constituency within the Islamic community did in fact consider it.

Surat-al-Jinn Q 72:1–19

In the name of God, the Merciful, the Compassionate.

The Jinn Hear the Qur'an[43]

Say: "I am inspired that a band of the jinn listened, and they said, 'Surely we have heard an amazing Qur'an! It guides to the right (course). We believe in it, and we shall not associate anyone with our Lord. And (we believe) that He—exalted (be) the majesty of our Lord!—He has not taken a consort or son. And that the foolish among us used to say an outrageous thing against God. And that we had thought that humans and jinn would never say any lie against God.'"

The Jinn Reminisce

And that individuals of humankind used to take refuge with individuals of the jinn, and they increased them in depravity. And that they thought as you (also) thought, that God will not raise up anyone. And that we touched the sky and found it filled with harsh guards and piercing flames [meteors–dp]. And that we used to sit there on seats to listen (in), but whoever listens now finds a piercing flame lying in wait for him. And that we do not know whether evil is intended for those who are on the earth, or whether their Lord intends right (guidance) for them.

---

43. This heading and others that follow within the quotations from Droge, trans., *The Qur'an*, are my additions.

The Jinn Reflect on their Future

And that some of us are righteous, and some of us are other than that—
we are on different roads. And that we (now) think that we shall not be
able to escape God on the earth, and shall not escape Him by flight. And
that when we heard the guidance, we believed in it, and whoever believes
in his Lord will not fear any deprivation or depravity. And that some of us
have submitted, and some of us are the ones who have deviated. Whoever
submits, those have sought out right (guidance), but as for the ones who
have deviated, they have become firewood for Gehenna!'" And (We say)
that if they had gone straight on the road, We would indeed have given
them water to drink in abundance, so that We might test them concerning
it. Whoever turns away from the remembrance of his Lord—He will place
him in hard punishment. And that the mosques (belong) to God, so do
not call on anyone (along) with God.

The Mysterious Nineteenth Verse

And that when the servant of God stood calling on Him, they were
almost upon him in hordes.

3

Surat-al-Jinn (The Jinn Sura)

Q 72:1–19—War in Heaven

Texts in Comparison: Genesis 3; Genesis 6;
1 Kings 22; Job 1, 2; Psalms 58; 82;
Isaiah 14; Ezekiel 28

Many religions describe a spiritual world different and somehow higher and more refined than the human world—invisible but deeply enmeshed in human activities and fate. One might find this invisible world in the sky, on the earth, or under the earth. The creatures inhabiting this world affect individual people and communities for both good and ill. Certain gifted humans have the ability to access this other world and bring back useful information to their community. For example, Surat-al-Bakara, the Cow Sura, describes two angels who brought divine messages:

> They taught the people magic, and what had been sent down to
> the two angels (in) Babylon. (Q 2:102)

In the Jewish tradition, the book of Enoch describes angelic powers called the Watchers, who bring wisdom to humanity.

> And Azazel taught men to make swords, and knives, and
> shields, and breastplates, and made known to them the metals
> of the earth and the art of working them, and bracelets, and
> ornaments, and the use of antimony, and the beautifying of the

47

eyelids, and all kinds of costly stones, and all colouring tinctures. And there arose much godlessness, and they committed fornication, and they were led astray, and became corrupt in all their ways. (Enoch 8)[1]

Many ancients pictured their universe in this way. However, the monotheisms of Judaism, Christianity, and Islam turned away from this view. Surprisingly, the differences between this old picture of the spiritual world and monotheism are more apparent than real. The monotheisms rejected this polytheistic universe in two ways. First, monotheism discounted the importance and even the presence of these alternate beings, insisting that only the one true God is important. Second, monotheisms denied the possibility that anything these other beings did or brought to humanity could help them.

In monotheism, the inhabitants of this spirit world are now distinguished from deity, no longer called gods. In the Bible and the Qur'an, the one God outshines all these other invisible supernatural beings. Notwithstanding the superiority of God, these others continue to move about in the scriptures and the traditions of Judaism, Christianity, and Islam—angels, devils, and many things in between. The intermediate ones, with their feet both on earth and in heaven had been uniquely charged to bring gifts and information from heaven (the nonhuman world) to the human realm. However, this service becomes suspect in this new monotheistic environment.

Ancient imaginations arranged otherworldly beings into hierarchies, much like the hierarchies the people experienced in everyday life. In the heavenly pantheon as on earth there were kings and royal families with offspring. There were servants and bureaucrats, and heavenly councils chaired by the King-God. Additionally, a group of in-between supernatural beings, neither divine nor human, appears in many East Mediterranean traditions. They inhabit a middle ground and mediate between the two realms, observing the doings of heaven, bringing messages back to earth. In a sense, they fill roles similar to the roles prophets occupy in the Israelite and Islamic traditions. Examples of intermediate beings include the *bene ha 'elohīm* in Genesis 6.[2] They were members of the heavenly council who raped human women.[3]

1. Charles, trans., *The Book of Enoch* in Charles et al., eds., *The Apocrypha*, n.p.

2. Literally, "sons of God," or "sons of *'elohīm*." In the Hebrew Bible *'elohīm* can either mean "gods" (plural) or "God" (singular). See the discussion of the *bene ha-'elohīm* in the Introduction.

3. The power differential between the sons of God and the human women was so great that their relations constitute rape.

The sons of God saw that they [the human women[4]] were fair; and
they took wives for themselves of all that they chose. (Gen 6:2)

In the book of Enoch, the heavenly Watchers bring secret knowledge to
the earthbound humans; In the Qur'an, the jinn are intermediate creatures.
In each religious tradition, these intermediate beings maintain an ambiguous identity. Were they angels? Demons? Demigods? Divine messengers?
Hypostases? The jinn are this kind of group found in the Qur'an and also in
ensuing Islamic narrative traditions.

On the Arabian Peninsula long before the advent of Islam, the people
regarded the jinn as members of the inaccessible spirit world. They could
fly, had great strength, and saw into the future. In that way they resembled
angels.[5] They lived near humans in parallel communities. Usually people
could not see them. They were liminal, that is, they lived in the margins
and the uninhabited places and represented the uncanny. It remains unclear
whether the jinn inhabit these places as a punishment for transgressions
(discussed below), or if such places are their natural habitation. Jinn were
regarded as sources of negativity and malignancy. In the stories of *The Thou-
sand and One Nights* (also called *The Arabian Nights*) people bound the jinn
with powerful spells and compelled them to serve human whims. In the
Qur'an, jinn served King Solomon.[6] The Arabic word for "crazy" is *maj-
noon*, which means, "possessed by jinn," or more literally, "jinnified." The
jinn appear to humans under extraordinary circumstances. Early Muslims
by virtue of their newfound commitment to monotheism, faced questions
about the jinn's status and power—questions that had not previously arisen.
They wondered how the jinn stood in relation to God; these early Muslims
rejected the notion of the jinn *as* gods. Their ancestors had believed that.
The verdict of the Qur'an, of course, is that the jinn cannot compete with
God, and have no power to improve the condition of the humans. Although
this verdict gives supremacy to God in a hierarchy of divine beings, it exists
in tension with the foundational Qur'anic idea, *tawḥid*, that there is only
one God.

There was a conflict between on the one hand those who believed that
the jinn were powerful and could actually help people, and on the other

4. Literally, "daughters of Adam" (*benōt ha'adam*).

5. In the Hebrew Bible and the New Testament, angels carry divine messages that
include predictions. In apocalyptic literature, angels bring veiled intimations about
future events. In Arabic (the Qur'an), in Hebrew (the Hebrew Bible), and in Greek (the
Septuagint and the New Testament), the word translated "angel" means "messenger."

6. These are places that describe how the jinn serve Solomon: Q 21:81–82; 27:38–40
(discussed in Chapter 6).

hand those who rejected the power of the jinn. The only record of the jinn comes from Muslim sources, and they are motivated to disparage the jinn and question their effectiveness. Previously there must have existed a positive case regarding the jinn. Such a case, although rejected by the Qur'an and by Islamic tradition, has left traces in the text. Although some pre-Islamic Arabian poetry mentions jinn, most of the data on them is seen through an Islamic lens. The Qur'anic treatment of the jinn, as Chabbi says, "is essentially defensive."[7] By that he means when the Qur'an writes about the jinn, it intends to reduce their influence. That determines how it represents them.

An examination of the Jinn Sura and the other passages about the jinn elsewhere in the Qur'an as well as a consideration of comparable places in the Hebrew Bible uncovers and highlights a basic narrative that underlies all these texts in both the Qur'an and the Bible. They each tell in some form a story about times when God punished divine beings who had sought to enlarge their place and bring secret information from heaven to humans. As we shall see, the defeat of the jinn in Surat-al-Jinn closely parallels the demotion of the *bene ha'elohīm* (members of the divine council) in the Hebrew Bible.

Although the Qur'an is usually sparse in narrative, and where narrative exists, sparse in detail, Surat-al-Jinn differs. More than most suras, it has a distinct narrative. Readers follow a series of connected events, each concerning jinn, the prophet Muhammad, and God. However, the Surat-al-Jinn story is not arranged chronologically. To further complicate the understanding, the story lacks a key plot element. This missing piece would have provided a very important part of the narrative puzzle. After the Qur'anic text was established in the form that now exists, the early interpreters endeavored to fill this gap using their imaginations. The *tafsīr*, the tradition of Qur'anic exegesis, connects the dots and supplies the missing information. I will examine this gap in the Qur'anic story and consider the various strategies by which later Islamic interpreters filled it.[8]

THE JINN STORY ARRANGED CHRONOLOGICALLY

In order to make sense of the narrative in Surat-al-Jinn, the reader must rearrange the verses, because the action begins in the middle and then goes backwards in the past and then skips ahead. In the opening scene, God

7. Chabbi, "Jinn," 46.

8. I am not examining the entire sura. Much of it (particularly the last section 20–28) only tangentially concerns the jinn.

commands the Prophet to report a vision he has received in which he sees a group of jinn having a discussion.

> A band of the jinn listened, and they said, "Surely we have heard an amazing Qur'an!" (Q 72:1)

These jinn discuss an event they have witnessed. They have heard "an amazing Qur'an." Subsequently, the reader discovers that the jinn had witnessed the Prophet himself chanting the Qur'an. Muhammad receives this vision of the jinn's conversation. The jinn describe the Prophet in some earlier time. In this vision given to the Prophet from his past, he stands at the center of the action. Three intertwined plots make up the narrative in the Jinn Sura. In the order of their appearance in the sura (not in chronological order), they are:

1. The Prophet receives a vision in which he sees a group of jinn having a discussion. The remainder of the narrative is told from the perspective of the overheard jinn. Muhammad listens in on the jinn. Oddly, later in the sura the jinn themselves are accused of listening in on privileged conversations.

2. In the discussion, the Prophet overhears the jinn recount that they have heard an excellent Qur'an.

3. This leads into the third level of narrative, and also the longest, and therefore probably the most important.

Here the jinn recount the story of the time when they were driven out of heaven.

> And that we touched the sky and found it filled with harsh guards and piercing flames. (Q 72:8)

The word translated "piercing flames" refers to meteors, with emphasis on their fiery appearance. (In parallel passages elsewhere in the Qur'an a different word is used, which emphasizes their aspect as projectiles.) There is no explanation in this sura as to why the jinn, having heard an excellent Qur'an, are as a result motivated to tell the story of when meteors chased them from the sky. This is the first of two major lacunae in the story, lacunae that later interpreters fill in and explain (see below). The third story has two parts—a before and an after. Before, the jinn enjoyed free access to heaven where they listened in on discussions in the divine council. After, whenever the jinn try to assume their accustomed places in heaven, they are driven out by flaming meteorites and strong guards.

To review: the first story is Muhammad's account of his vision of a collection of jinn. The second story is the content of the jinn's discussion, which is that at a previous time they had heard "an amazing Qur'an," that is, they had heard Muhammad reciting some part of the Qur'an. The third story is what the jinn say about their previous experiences when they sat in, listening to discussions in the divine council and were driven out.

The jinn recollect what would have been placed first if the story were told chronologically. They fondly recall the time before they lost their status, a time when they had free access to heaven; but something happened to change all that.

> And that we used to sit there on seats to listen (in) but whoever
> listens now finds a piercing flame lying in wait for him. (Q 72:9)

I will address the "harsh guards" and "piercing flames" later. For now, I focus on the former status of the jinn, before the advent of these impediments. They had seats in heaven for purposes of listening in on discussion in the divine council. When this same story is picked up in another sura, it uses the word for eavesdropping, a phrase which literally means, "to steal the hearing":

> Certainly We have made constellations in the sky, and made it
> appear enticing for the onlookers, and protected it from every
> accursed satan [i.e., the jinn]—except any who (may) *steal in
> to overhear*, then a clear flame pursues him. (Q 15:16–18, ital-
> ics added)

Subsequent interpretations of the Jinn Sura also impose this idea of illicit listening, but the Jinn Sura does not say that. Rather, the sura describes the jinn as regularly seated in assigned spots from which they observe divine consultations. The jinn have taken these seats in heaven on many occasions. They used to go to these designated places and would thereby keep apprised of angelic gossip and listen in on divine strategy sessions. This story changes in later interpretation.[9] They are called "evil satans" in Q 37:

> And (We have made them) [the meteors] a (means of) pro-
> tection from every rebellious satan. They do not listen to the
> exalted Assembly, but they are pelted from every side, driven
> off—for them (there is) punishment forever. (Q 37:7–9)

---

9. I assume it was written later because it is more in conformity with Islamic orthodoxy. There is no conclusive reason why it could have been contemporary or even earlier.

It embarrassed and disturbed the ancient Islamic commentators to imagine that these jinn, usually badly behaved creatures, at one time had access to the heavenly realm. These subsequent versions are particularly sensitive to any taint that might reflect badly upon God's domicile. They concluded that if at some point these disreputable jinn had visited heaven, they must have breached divine protocol, appearing like a stain on a beautiful garment. They could have only secretly gained entrance without permission. They were eavesdropping where they did not belong. According to later interpretation, when the jinn in sura 72 (and its parallels) complain about the piercing flame, they speak only of an *increase* in the number of meteors. According to these interpreters, there had always been meteors. For the jinn to listen in to the divine council was always wrong (they say)—it is only that God eventually stepped up his enforcement to bar uninvited access. The jinn had never been welcome in heaven, and any access they may have had in the past was illegitimate and transgressed previously established boundaries. In this new protocol, God decided to crack down on such trespassing. That was the only thing that changed. In another sura, God says,

> Certainly we adorned the lower heaven with lamps, and made
> them missiles for the satans. (Q 67:5)

There is a similarity between this story and an account at the beginning of the book of Job. In both cases there is a divine figure or figures (the Satan[10] in Job, the jinn in the Qur'an) with access to heaven. In the Qur'an the jinn are kicked out. In the book of Job, the Satan is not kicked out, but the narrator treats him separately.

> One day the heavenly beings came to present themselves before
> the LORD, and [the] Satan also came among them. (Job 1:6; See
> also Job 2:1)

Elsewhere in the Bible (see below) a Satan figure is in fact kicked out of heaven. In Job, the Satan had unrestricted divine access.

Regarding the jinn, a 1980 translation of vv. 9 and 10 of the Jinn Sura by Muhammad Asad uses brackets to indicate what he adds to the Arabic text to explain it:

> Notwithstanding that we were established in positions [which
> we had thought well-suited] to listening to [whatever secrets
> might be in] it. (Q 72:9)

---

10. The definite article in the Hebrew is seldom translated. Including the definite article makes *hasaṭan* ("the one who opposes") not a name but an office.

This is Yusuf Ali's translation from 1934. He adds parentheses to indicate his interpretive additions:

> We used, indeed, to sit there in (hidden) stations, to (steal) a hearing. (Q 72:9)

Dawood uses no parentheses or brackets—just raw paraphrase. He changes the word "listening" to "eavesdropping":

> We sat eavesdropping . . .

In each case, the translator took what was a neutral term in Arabic, meaning "to sit" or "to abide," and made it into something underhanded and dishonest, "eavesdropping" or "stealing."

In vv. 8–9, the jinn reminisce about their previous privileged access. Formerly, before something happened that changed their status, they had regular places in heaven from which they listened. The early Islamic interpreters were wrong. Previously, the jinn had a place in heaven. Their loss of status and access caused their agitation. After they had listened, the jinn brought this information back to their human clients. In v. 6, Droge translates as follows:

> And that individuals of humankind used to take refuge with individuals of the jinn, and they [the jinn] increased them [humanity] in depravity. (Q 72:6)

Humans sought benefit from the jinn. Other suras confirm that the people worshiped jinn. They recognized the jinn's superiority in power and wisdom, and perhaps they adored their divine magnificence. The Qur'an provides ample evidence of this. Consider these verses:

> They make the jinn associates[11] with God, when He created them, and they assign to Him sons and daughters without any knowledge. (Q 6:100)

> They will say "Glory to You! You are our ally, not they." No! They used to serve the jinn—most of them believed in them. (Q 34:41)

> They have fabricated an affiliation between Him and the jinn. Yet certainly the jinn know that they will indeed be brought forward (to the punishment). (Q 37:158)

11. This is a verbal form of *shirk*, meaning "to associate." The sura uses a form of the word *shirk*, commonly used to condemn either comparing God to something lesser or, in this case, calling something lesser God.

When the jinn sat in their seats in heaven, to what exactly did they listen? A biblical text supplies an answer to this question. The jinn were listening in on the divine council, the meeting God convenes with the angels, the assembly where they determine human fate. One finds divine councils (places and times where the gods discuss important matters) in many ancient Mediterranean mythologies. Certain subsidiary gods, demigods, or other intermediaries between the heavenly world and humans listen in. Then they bring knowledge from these councils to aid humans. For instance, in the Hebrew Bible, King Ahab hires Michaiah ben Imlah, an Israelite prophet, to discern Yahweh's intentions concerning an upcoming battle. The prophet describes how he listened in on the battle plans of Yahweh and his lieutenants, here called spirits. This is Yahweh's divine council:

> I saw the LORD sitting on his throne, with all the host of heaven standing beside him to the right and to the left of him. And the LORD said, "Who will entice Ahab, so that he may go up and fall at Ramoth-gilead?" Then one said one thing, and another said another, until a spirit came forward and stood before the LORD, saying, "I will entice him." (1 Kgs 22:19–22)

The prophet Michaiah observes heavenly conversations, as do the jinn in the sura, and they both brought this information back to earth. The role of the prophet and the role of the jinn are similar. In the aforementioned account at the beginning of the book of Job, the *bene ha'elohīm* (literally "sons of the god" or "sons of the gods") gather together in heaven, taking their seats in an assembly.

> One day the heavenly beings came to present themselves before the LORD, and [the] Satan also came among them. (Job 1:6)

This assemblage resembles the jinn when they sat in their heavenly listening seats. The biblical account does not distinguish individual *bene ha'eloīm*. Similarly, the Qur'anic narrative treats the jinn collectively. The sura neither names them nor distinguishes them from one another. The Satan however is set apart in the book of Job:

> . . . [the] Satan also came among them. (Job 1:6)

In Greek mythology, the gods punish Prometheus for bringing fire to the humans.[12] In the book of Enoch, the Watchers bring gifts and knowledge from their heavenly realm. They too are punished. The punishment of the jinn fits right in as a version of the same story.

---

12. See also the Sumerian Ea/Enki.

THE MISSING EVENT

The jinn enjoyed unrestricted access to heaven. At some point, something happened that ends this idyllic situation. Whatever it is that happens, as a result the jinn lose access to heaven and so can no longer help the humans with valued information. The sura gives no hint at what this epochal event might have been that caused their banishment. An examination of parallel passages in the Bible clarifies the story. Rather than the absence one finds in the Qur'an, one finds in the Hebrew Bible through its parallel passages two distinct suggested explanations as to why heavenly beings might be expelled from heaven. First, Genesis 6 it says of the *bene ha 'elohīm*:

> The sons of God [*bene ha 'elohīm*] saw that the they [human women] [*benôt ha 'Adam*][13] were fair; and they took wives for themselves of all that they chose. (Gen 6:2)

In Genesis this angelic transgression—angels having sex with human women—results in the worldwide flood described in Genesis chapters 6–9. There is, however, an alternate version of angelic malfeasance, found most explicitly in Psalms 58 and 82. In these psalms, the intermediate beings do not transgress sexual taboos as in Genesis 6 but rather engage in misgovernance.[14]

> Do you indeed decree what is right, you gods [*'elohīm*]?
>   Do you judge people fairly?
> No, in your hearts you devise wrongs;
>   your hands deal out violence on earth. (Ps 58:1–2)

In Psalm 82, in addition to the term *'elohīm,* beings are called *bene 'elyōn,* "children of *'Elyōn." 'Elyōn* is usually translated "most high." Thus the phrase is rendered "children of the Most High." In this psalm, Yahweh accuses these *'elohīm* of injustice, and therefore banishes them and makes them mortal.

> I say, "You are gods [*'elohīm*],
>   children of the Most High [*bene 'elyōn*], all of you;
> nevertheless, you shall die like mortals,
>   and fall like any prince." (Ps 82:6–7)

There is a narrative that underlies these two psalms and some other passages as well. Isaiah and Ezekiel form from this same underlying narrative their judgment against boastful kings cast down from their high places.

---

13. The NRSV does not translate the noun "daughters of *adam*," and just says, "the sons of God saw that *they* were fair."

14. See Penchansky, *Twilight,* chapters 3 and 4.

Both Isaiah and Ezekiel use the details of this ancient story to frame a criticism against a king who is their contemporary. From Isaiah:

> [You said] "I will ascend to the tops of the clouds,
> > I will make myself like the Most High ['elyōn]."
> But you are brought down to Sheol,
> > to the depths of the Pit. (Isa 14:14–15)

And Ezekiel, writing about a different king at a different time, but with a similar theme says,

> You were on the holy mountain of God;
> > you walked among the stones of fire.
> You were blameless in your ways
> > from the day that you were created . . .
> [Then] I cast you as a profane thing from the mountain of God,
> > and the guardian cherub drove you out
> > from among the stones of fire. (Ezek 28:16)

Some traces of this ancient narrative remain in these two diatribes. "Stones of fire" at first seems to describe a heavenly, bejeweled highway. But the stones of fire might be stars or meteors. Then the phrase "drove out from among stones of fire" in Ezekiel would be very close to the flaming meteors thrown at the jinn in the Jinn Sura.

> And that we touched the sky and found it filled with harsh guards and piercing flames. (Q 72:8)

This Qur'anic verse mentioned earlier gives further details:

> Surely we have made the sky of this world appear enticing by means of the splendor of the stars, and (We have made them) a (means of) protection from every rebellious satan. They do not listen to the exalted Assembly, but are pelted from every side, driven off. (Q 37:7)

"Rebellious satan" in Q 37 is an alternate name for the beings called the jinn in the Jinn Sura. The jinn are often called satans in the Qur'an. In another sura Satan (here called Iblis[15]) is called a jinn:

> (Remember) when We said to the angels, "Prostrate yourself before Adam," and they prostrated themselves, except Iblis. He was one of the jinn. (Q 18:50)

---

15. Iblis is thought to be a shortened form of the Greek term *diabolos*.

The stars in Q 37 function the way the meteors do in Ezekiel 28: These fiery projectiles serve to keep out the intermediate beings, whether these beings are called *'elohīm* in the Bible or rebellious satans in the Qur'an. Consider this passage.

> Certainly We adorned the lower heaven with lamps, and made them missiles[16] for the satans . . . (Q 67:5)

This same ancient narrative where supernatural beings are cast out of heaven, lies behind the enigmatic words of Jesus in the Gospel of Luke:

> I watched Satan fall from heaven like a flash of lightening.
> (Luke 10:18)

In the biblical accounts of angelic misbehavior in Genesis and the Psalms, the transgression is so heinous that it puts the universe out of balance. In Genesis, the *'elohīm* had raped human women. In Psalms 58 and 82, they governed corruptly. God rectifies this imbalance by initiating a major shift in the world's governance. In Genesis, God unmakes the world, sending a flood, murdering almost everyone. In the two psalms, Yahweh deposes former gods and declares that Yahweh is sole judge. In spite of the parallels between the biblical accounts and the Jinn Sura, there is no corresponding violation by the jinn against God in the Qur'anic account. Its absence constitutes a significant rupture in the narrative. What could the jinn have done equally heinous so that it caused the heavenly gates to close against them?

When the Jinn Sura is contrasted to the biblical versions, it is odd that the sura does not mention a transgressive event that would have caused the jinn's dislocation. The early Islamic tradition quickly supplies the missing information. Commentators claim that the jinn lost access at the time because that was the moment when the Prophet began to receive his revelations. Since the Prophet brought the final message from heaven, there was no longer any need for other sources of or means by which to obtain divine information. Early interpreters claim that the presence of the final prophet and the final revelation (the Qur'an) transform the organization of the universe. One of the changes in the new order is that whatever function jinn might have had to bring divine information to humans, humans did not need them any longer. The Qur'an is sufficient to discern God's desires and intentions.

---

16. This is different from the word "piercing flames," which emphasizes the flaming nature of the object. In this sura, the word used emphasizes the object as a projectile, something thrown, so "missile" is the best translation. The two words refer to different aspects of the same phenomenon.

However, this elaborate argument, creating a relationship between the banishment of jinn and the coming of the Prophet is spurious. There is no hint of it in the sura. The absence of a reason for the jinn banishment remains as a serious irritant. An alternative explanation (although the interpreters are not able to keep these two interpretations separate) is that the jinn were *never* welcome in heaven. From the beginning they had somehow snuck in. The reason they are banished is that their subterfuge is discovered. Their banishment did not signal a change in policy: the jinn had *always* been prohibited from heaven but had insinuated themselves in some dark corner of the heavenly council chambers while nobody was looking. They truly were eavesdropping. Q 38 refers to the council, the site of the jinn's "listening seats." The Prophet is speaking:

> I had no knowledge of the exalted Assembly when they disputed. (Q 38:69)

Either heaven banishes the jinn because of the coming of the Qur'an, or else they had always been intruders. In order for either interpretation to stand, the gap (the absence of a cause for the jinn banishment) must be filled in with a plausible scenario, and an explanation must be given for why such a scenario is not part of the Qur'anic account. Following this unmentioned event, whatever it was, heaven tightens things up and becomes stricter about who will gain access to the divine assembly. The strong guards clear out heaven's visitor galleries of these now unwelcome liminal beings.

> [The jinn] found it [heaven] filled with harsh guards and piercing flames. (Q 72:8)

None of the early commentators can demonstrate a link that might connect the coming of the Prophet and the banishment of the jinn. Why had it been acceptable for the jinn to go to heaven *before* Muhammad's time, while afterwards the angels barred the way? Neither the sura nor the tradition that surrounds it ever adequately answers this question.

In contrast to the Jinn Sura, in Q 37 these figures are demonized quite literally. But the basic story remains. They are driven out of heaven by flaming projectiles. In summary, most Islamic interpreters credit Muhammad's prophecy as the direct cause of the jinn's loss of status. However, the sura itself does not suggests that the Prophet's coming changes the status of the jinn. The only evidence for such a connection is that the jinn describe a time when they heard Muhammad chanting the Qur'an:

> Surely we have heard an amazing Qur'an! (Q 72:1)

The juxtaposition of Muhammad chanting the Qur'an and the jinn's recollection of banishment suggest to some that the one caused the other. On the contrary, the sura does not in any way suggest that *because* the Prophet brought the Qur'an, God kicked the jinn out of heaven. The missing plot element that caused God to remove the jinn from heaven remains unspoken, a glaring absence.

Why does the sura choose not to speak of this missing plot element? Some possible combination of the following reasons might explain the omission: First, perhaps the sura assumes that everyone knows the story, so there us no need to speak of this missing plot element. Second, maybe the sura needs only allude to the jinn banishment in order for the original readers and hearers to provide all the necessary details. The Qur'an commonly makes such allusions when referring to familiar stories from other sources. (See Chapter 7.) Or, third, perhaps the gap might be a deliberate obfuscation in the Qur'an. The author might have tried to conceal or obfuscate the reason for the jinn banishment in order to avoid an uncomfortable truth. Such a deliberate ambiguity papers over tensions or contradictions between the Jinn Sura's picture of the world, and the world picture of emerging orthodoxy. If we assume the author has made the text deliberately obscure, such obscurity frees up the meaning and make the story subject to diverse interpretations. This might have been the intention. Consider another possibility—that the missing piece is unknown, but that the story as it now exists is too well-known and sacred to be changed or added to. Alternatively, what seems a gap to contemporary readers might have seemed perfectly whole to ancient readers in ways we can no longer comprehend. Finally, the text might be missing key pieces that for some reason dropped out in the process of transmission.

If we rearrange the story elements chronologically, it begins when the jinn have open access to heaven in their "listening seats," and they bring from heaven important information. Then something happens. As a result, heaven has suddenly instituted a new policy, having given no warning or explanation beforehand, which forbids the jinn to sit in their listening posts. Henceforth, if they fly up to heaven to take their accustomed places, strong guards and flaming meteors bar their way. This image recalls a text older than the Qur'an, where an angel and a flaming sword bars the way to paradise (Gen 3):

> He drove out the man; and at the east of the garden of Eden he
> placed the cherubim, and a sword flaming and turning to guard
> the way to the tree of life." (Gen 3:24)

Recall the passage in Ezekiel mentioned earlier:

> The guardian cherub drove you out
> from among the stones of fire. (Ezek 28:16)

The angel in Genesis corresponds to the strong guards in the Jinn Sura and to the guarding cherubim in Ezekiel. The flaming sword in Genesis corresponds to the meteors in the Jinn Sura and to the stones of fire in Ezekiel:

Genesis 3	Ezekiel	Jinn Sura
cherubim	guardian cherub	strong guards
flaming sword	stones of fire	piercing flames (meteors)

One must not forget that there is more to the Jinn Sura than this story of the jinn driven from heaven. In the first section, the jinn overhear the Prophet reciting the Qur'an. Although both these scenes concern jinn, there is no necessary or explicit connection between them, one that makes narrative sense of their placement together. The early Islamic traditions make this connection by filling in plot details. In the fabricated story, the jinn, blindsided by the meteors and angelic guards, form a delegation to roam the earth, commissioned to determine the reason why heaven has banished them. In one version of the story, Iblis, that is, Satan, here described as leader of the jinn, is the one who appoints and commissions this delegation. It is during their mission that the jinn overhear the Prophet reciting the Qur'an and they are struck with its excellence:

> A band of jinn listened . . . and said, "Surely we have heard an amazing Qur'an!" (Q 72:1)

Then they declare their submission to God:

> We believe in it [the Qur'an], and we shall not associate anyone with our Lord. (Q 72:2–3)

From the Jinn Sura and traditional additions, the following plot line emerges:

> At one time, the jinn enjoyed access to the divine council, and they divulged to humans secret information they overheard. Then suddenly, without explanation, God's guards violently drive them away from their appointed seats. The doors of heaven are slammed shut against them. When they try to re-enter, fiery meteors assail them, and strong angelic guards bar their way. Even though the people on earth, the humans, are desperate for the information that the jinn have provided, the jinn no longer have any information to offer. A delegation of jinn is therefore commissioned to comb the earth for evidence that might

account for their change in status. While on this journey, the jinn came upon the Prophet as he leads his followers in prayer. They are struck with the wisdom and eloquence of what they are hearing and became Muslims on the spot. They subsequently bring the message of Islam back to the other jinn.

THE CURIOUS CASE OF VERSE 19

Verse 19 brings this jinn narrative to screeching halt. This enigmatic verse places the interpretation of the entire sura in doubt. Its ambiguities cause one to question the dominant narrative (see above), in which compliant jinn become Muslim when they encounter the Prophet. Just as in verse 1, so in verse 19 the Prophet prays before an audience. It is in fact the same incident, described twice, the second time with more details. In Droge's translation:

> And that when the servant of God stood calling on Him, they were almost upon him in hordes. (Q 72:19)

The Arabic literally means,

> ... they were almost upon him crowding/smothering. (my trans.)

Translator Asad adds a good deal to make v. 19 more orthodox. For Asad, the verse is not about the jinn at all. The bracketed phrases provided by Asad indicate his additions:

> Yet [thus it is] that whenever a servant of God stands up in prayer to him, they [who are bent on denying the truth] would gladly overwhelm him with their crowds.

Ali's translation:

> Yet when the Devotee of Allah stands forth to invoke him, they crowded.

Some have suggested that "they" are the unbelievers who sought to disrupt the Prophet's prayers on many occasions. I found one source claiming that "they" are the believers crowding around the Prophet to catch his every word.

Again, the literal meaning of the verse is,

> They were all over him, nearly smothering him. (my trans.)

The word in Arabic for "crowding" or "smothering," *libad'an*, originally described densely curled strands of wool, and elsewhere describes thickly gathered clouds. Smothering threatens the Prophet. In one *tafsīr*, the Prophet is described as completely obscured from view, only his up-raised hand visible. Another *tafsīr* describes the swarm as like a flock of birds. Some interpreters rather claim that a crowd of admirers surrounds the Prophet, but whether out of enthusiasm for his teaching, or because they seek to bully and frighten him, the Prophet is almost lost in the crowd. There is a strong and chilling resemblance here to the description of the gods crowding around the sacrifice at the end of the *Gilgamesh* flood story.

> Then I let out (all) to the four winds
> And offered a sacrifice . . .
> The gods smelled the savor.
> The gods smelled the sweet savor.
> The gods crowded like flies about the sacrifice.[17]

The scene of jinn surrounding the Prophet resembles the grotesque picture of the gods surrounding the sacrifice in *Gilgamesh*. Perhaps the jinn think they might feed on the Prophet the way that the gods in *Gilgamesh* are hungry for the sacrificial meat. Likewise, in the book of Enoch, the Watch-ers, intermediate beings like the jinn, swarm around Enoch, begging him to defend them in the divine court.

> And they besought me to draw up a petition for them that they
> might find forgiveness, and to read their petition in the presence
> of the Lord of heaven. For from thenceforward they could not
> speak (with Him) nor lift up their eyes to heaven for shame of
> their sins for which they had been condemned. Then I wrote
> out their petition, and the prayer in regard to their spirits and
> their deeds individually and in regard to their requests that they
> should have forgiveness and length (of days). (Enoch 13:4–6)[18]

Verse 19 of the Jinn Sura does not identify "God's servant," the one who is praying. There are different theories as to his identity. It might be a generic reference to a believer, a Muslim, one who submits. However, the name "God's servant" is frequently used in the Qur'an to refer to the Prophet Muhammad. Because v. 1 and v. 19 refer to the same event, v. 19 likely refers to the Prophet.

The jinn surround the Prophet. "Smothering" (*libad'an*) implies vio-lence, and in this context is life-threatening. The Prophet is not actually be-ing smothered at this moment. Rather, he is *almost* smothered, surrounded by crowds of eager jinn. The threat existed that Muhammad might be

---

17 Speiser, *Ancient Near Eastern Texts*, 60–72.

18. Charles, trans., *The Book of Enoch*, in Charles et al., eds., *The Apocrypha*, n.p.

overwhelmed by these crowds. The violence had not actually happened yet. The "they" in the sentence "*they* nearly smothered him" are the jinn, who have been the topic of the sura from the beginning. The two verses, 1 and 19, align in their similarity of place (a place of prayer), their similarity of action (prayer with outsiders watching), and their similarity of actors (Muhammad and the jinn). The sura is mostly about the jinn, and there is no strong reason to think that the jinn are not the main actors in v. 19.

When the jinn hear the Prophet reciting the Qur'an, they say:

> We believe in it [the Qur'an] and we shall not associate anyone
> with our Lord. (Q 72:2)

The jinn in these first few verses are placid and pious. In contrast, the jinn in v. 19 threaten the Prophet. If all the jinn had been as easy to convince as they appeared to be in v. 1, there would have been no need for the meteors and the strong guards. In that case, polite and firm refusal would have sufficed to keep the jinn out of heaven. But no, heaven brings the heavy artillery, flaming projectiles hurtling toward the miscreants. The two verses, 1 and 19, stand in sharp contrast. In v. 1, the jinn hear and immediately believe. In v. 19 they nearly smother the Prophet. There are indeed other hints in the sura of jinn hostility toward God and God's servants. The reaction from heaven, which sends meteors and posts strong guards, is disproportionate to the sin of trespassing. It suggests that God is in fact responding to a more aggressive assault against heavenly battlements. The jinn have done more than mere "listening." Therein lies the missing puzzle piece. In further evidence, the jinn speak of their attempt to escape from God:

> And that we (now) think that we shall not be able to escape God
> on the earth, and shall not escape Him by flight. (Q 72:12)

Why would the jinn need to escape from God? This additional verse puts in context the notion of the jinn attacking (or threatening to attack) Muhammad while he prays (Q 72:19).

Clearly the attack on the Prophet, if that is what it was, is a different event than the war in heaven, which is the narrative that underlies the sura. The war in heaven (unmentioned in the sura) and the attack on the Prophet (which is mentioned) are part of the same impulse, and are meant to comment on each other. It is similar to how the two kings in the Isaiah and Ezekiel prophecies reproduce the rebellion of the angel against God.

This scenario where hordes of hostile jinn surround the Prophet suggests a reason for the jinns' enforced banishment from heaven. Because v. 19 is included in the story, we get this: The jinn are still compelled to submit to God, but not before they try to resist divine authority. In a striking parallel,

I note the cosmic struggle between Yahweh and the chaos monsters, which lies behind the narrative and poetry of Genesis, Exodus, Job, and many psalms. Referring to God, the poets write,

> Was it not you who cut Rahab in pieces,
>   who pierced the dragon? (Isa 51:9)

> By his power he stilled the sea,
>   by his understanding he struck down Rahab. (Job 26:12).[19]

Psalms 58 and 82 recount the struggle between Yahweh and the 'elohīm. A similar struggle between God and the jinn in Surat-al-Jinn and its parallels would explain why God banishes the jinn. The attempted violence against the Prophet, God's messenger, is a trace of the unspoken violence against God.

The Jinn Sura skillfully brings two disparate worldviews together—first, the worldview where a single power, God, controls all; and, second, a worldview where God struggles for power against the jinn. Muslims opt for the first because they do not associate anything with God. God stands alone in power, authority, excellences, and virtues. The Islamic God tends toward a model of deity that we might call Aristotelean—that is, God is that which no greater can be conceived. But there is this other, suggesting a past struggle for dominance where God supplants other supernatural forces. The Hebrew Bible presents a God full of faults—a God who becomes angry, who can be thwarted, and who makes impossible demands. Islam affirms the perfect, all-sufficient God. The existence of the jinn challenge the Islamic notion of God. There were three ways the Qur'an could reconcile *tawhid* with the presence of the jinn. First, it could declare that the jinn did not exist. For example, in sura 53 the three "daughters of God" are declared to be mere words. (See Chapter 2.)

> They are only names you have named. (Q 53:23)

Alternatively, the Qur'an could declare the jinn demonic, part of the evil forces arrayed against God. In the Q 37:6–10, which appears to be a later version of the story found first in the Jinn Sura, the jinn are called "rebellious satans." Q 37 demonizes the jinn. However, this strategy (equating the jinn with demons) is not the way Surat-al-Jinn establishes God's supremacy. In this sura one finds a third strategy. Muslims may keep the jinn around, but the Qur'an promulgates a story that renders the jinn powerless and subservient.

19. See also Job 41 (Leviathan); Job 9:13; Ps 89:10.

This strategy transformed the older traditions regarding the jinn, which were well-known in the region. It also provided continuity between older beliefs and the new religious ideas introduced by Muhammad. By diminishing the jinn, the Jinn Sura accomplishes two things; it maintains God (wih a capital G) as the only supreme power, and it does not disturb the pre-Islamic Arabic hierarchy of cosmic beings. The Arabic audience of the Prophet's message believed in this hierarchy. The people could still have the jinn as denizens of the in-between world and yet maintain their monotheism. This sura thus decenters and displaces this powerful heavenly subgroup, the jinn. The Qur'anic author chooses this strategy because the belief in the jinn had important functions in the culture of the Arab people. It was woven into their daily life through rituals and figures of speech. The Qur'an's tolerance of jinn justified and explained the people's fear of liminal places—places they believed were haunted by the jinn. Surat-al-Jinn asks and answers the following question: How is it possible to regard God as the one true power when there also exist these powerful spirit beings, the jinn? The sura answers by portraying the powerful God defeating the jinn and taking away all their power, as Yahweh took away the power of the 'elohīm (Pss 58; 82).

The Qur'an reflects the ancient story. The jinn compete with God for the attention, loyalty, and dependence of the people. This is a newer version of the ancient mythic struggle that determines dominance between divine beings. The victor becomes the supreme God when he (always a he!) deposes his competitors and casts them out of heaven.

You can have your jinn, the sura tells the early Islamic community, but know that they will have no power. Chabbi describes them as "figures whose effective role has been considerably curtailed."[20] They have no special knowledge, no ability to help. If the people resort to them, the jinn will only confuse them.

> And that individuals of humankind used to take refuge with
> individuals of the jinn, and they increased them in depravity.
> (Q 72:6)

Of course the sura's account comes from the winning side in the struggle for dominance, the party of strict monotheism. The sura portrays a cowering and pious jinn abjectly capitulating to God's supreme power. When read through this lens, the band of jinn in v. 1 who quickly convert portray the demoralized shreds of jinn society suing for peace.

Surat al-Jinn organizes the inhabitants of the invisible world in accordance with the Islamic belief in the oneness of God. Before the advent of

20. Chabbi, "Jinn" 43.

Islam, the jinn received worship and they helped people. They had access to the heavenly courts. But now they are obsequious and powerless. The *bene-ha- 'elohīm* are similarly demoted Israelite heavenly beings. The jinn before demotion might have been gods of the desert. Now God has demoted them to quasi-divine status: they are intermediate beings, not divine; having both material and metaphysical qualities, though not divine. Thus, they retell a common story of beings cast out of heaven. The ones cast out of heaven are older figures of worship rejected by a new and emerging religious consensus. The story of the conversion of the jinn becomes an allegorical way to embody Islam's challenge to and victory over older religious ideas.

These two manifestations of beings cast out of heaven, in the Qur'an and the Bible, are different in many ways. Their similarities do not arise because the Qur'an copied the Bible. Nor can the similarities be coincidental. Rather, the Bible and the Qur'an share this mythological story on a deep level. The two holy books are close in geography but distant in time, and a similar plotline emerges in both. These stories of rebellious deities retain a stubborn existence in the religious traditions that replace them.

Part 2

The Problem of Theodicy

S hall not the judge of all the earth do what is just? (Gen 18:25).
Theodicy comes from two words, one meaning "God" (from the Greek *theos*) and the other "justification," (from *dikaiasunē*). *Theodicy* describes a field in theology that tries to justify God's behavior. But why does God need to be justified? Theodicy addresses "the problem of evil." Evil is a problem for the monotheist who believes that God is all good and all-powerful. An all-good God would desire to eliminate evil and suffering. An all-powerful God has the ability to do so. How then can evil exist if God is all good and all-powerful? These two attributes (goodness and omnipotence) should make the existence of evil impossible. An all-powerful and benevolent God can eradicate evil and would want to. How then can we explain the existence of evil while at the same time maintaining belief in monotheism? That briefly sets forth the problem of evil. Another way to express this problem asks, Why do bad things happen to good people? Either God does not care about suffering or is too weak to truly help people. Since the presence of evil is unmistakable,[1] the problem appears intractable.

---

1. Both Buddhism and Christian Science claim that evil is illusory. St. Augustine refused to recognize evil as an existing thing, but rather only the corruption of the good.

It is a particularly acute problem for monotheists. Polytheists or dualists can always blame an evil god for all their troubles.

These three chapters examine the various strategies in the Qur'an and in corresponding biblical passages that address the problem of evil. Monotheists have developed answers. Some accept that God has evil tendencies. Others blame human disobedience and free will as the cause of all human suffering. Others blame Satan.

Neither the Bible nor the Qur'an considered these options. For them, evil is palpable.

Surat-al-Masad Q 111

In the name of God, the Merciful, the Compassionate. The hands of Abu Lahab have perished, and he has perished. His wealth and what he has earned were of no use to him. He will burn in a flaming Fire, and his wife (will be) the carrier of the firewood, with a rope of fiber around her neck.

4

Surat-al-Masad (The Fiber)

Q 111:1–5—Abu Lahab's Curse

Texts in Comparison: Genesis 18:25; Exodus 15:1;
Deuteronomy 28:48; 2 Kings 2:23–24; Psalm 137; 139:22;
James 5:1–3; Revelation 19:3

Surat-al-Masad, the Palm Leaf Sura, stands unique in the Qur'an because it curses a single, named individual who appears to have been a contemporary of the Prophet. Abu Lahab, the subject of the sura, is wealthy and married. Q 111 curses him to fiery torments. These torments take place in hell. The name Abu Lahab in Arabic means "father of flames." (Hell is referred to as *lahab* in Q 77:31 and Q 111:3.) Some say Muhammad called him Father of Flames because he kept the votive flame burning before the statue of Uzza. Thus tradition names him Abdul-Uzza. In that case, Abu Lahab would not be a name but rather a description of his nature and his fate as one whose future it is to be burned.[1] Indeed the moniker Father of Flames aptly describes his fate: to burn in fire.[2] As a result of the history-rootedness of the sura, it has more connections to seventh-century Arabia than many other parts of the Qur'an. By rootedness I mean to contrast it with suras that seek a more universal stance, and to contrast it too with those that narrate a distant past. The history of the interpretation of this sura

1. It parallels Saint Paul calling Satan "the son of perdition" (2 Thess 2:3 KJV).
2. The Assad translation (1980) is "him with the glowing countenance."

73

portrays a complex relationship between the sacred text and the communities that interpret it. The sura supports the notion that bad people suffer or will suffer in hell, and that is one kind of theodicy. All who suffer deserve it, or put another way, every single human act will receive its corresponding reward or punishment.

The sura is short, just five verses. It begins:

> Oh, that the accomplishments[3] of Abu Lahab would be completely destroyed,[4]
> What good will his prosperity do him then?[5] (my trans.)

Some things are oddly missing from the sura, missing because one expects them to be there. First, the sura gives no hint regarding the identity of Abu Lahab. Second, there is no mention of what Abu Lahab has done to deserve such punishment. Finally, aside from the formulaic opening, the bismillah, the sura never mentions God.[6] The sura implies that God is the one who punishes Abu Lahab for unspecified sins by casting him into hell. But it is unusual for a chapter of the Qur'an not to mention God explicitly.

In the third verse, which reads,

> He will burn in a fire of flame. (Q 111:3; my trans.)

three different words are used that in some way indicate burning: *sayaṣla*, the future form of the verb "to burn"; *n'ar'an*, "a fire"; and *lahab*, "flame." The last word, *lahab*, is the same as in the name in the first verse, Abu Lahab, "father of flames."

Abu Lahab's wife takes center stage in the last two verses. She carries firewood and wears woven palm fibers (*masad*) on her neck. Is it a necklace? A yoke? An animal's collar? The sura does not say. In spite of what one finds in many common translations and interpretations, the Arabic text of the sura does not include a word about collars, necklaces, or yokes. Literally, one reads,

> On her neck, plaited palm fibers (*masad*). (Q 111:5; my trans.)

---

3. Literally "hands," as a metonym for power.

4. I am ignoring the double verb here, more properly translated as "Perish the hands of Abu Lahab, and perish he." Some have discussed the subtle differences between these two subphrases, but I see it as a hendiadys and an intensification.

5. There is a double noun here not translated: "his wealth and all he has gained." Once again, I see intensification and hendiadys.

6. The bismillah ("In the Name of God the Merciful and Compassionate") was added later.

Why is the wife of Abu Lahab described as a carrier of firewood? Here are four possibilities:

1. The term is merely descriptive. Abu Lahab's wife gathers firewood for her husband, a common household arrangement. It would therefore not be a curse but a colorful description.

2. Some suggest that "carrying firewood" is a way to describe gossiping, carrying tales. The phrase would then become a description of her character, and not part of the curse.

3. Abu Lahab's unnamed wife was a highborn woman, and the curse upon her requires her to do the job of a menial laborer, carrying the family's fuel.

In order to make sense of the sura, these three interpretations each divide the sura into *two* stories—one that describes Abu Lahab suffering in hell, and a the second that describes his wife carrying wood in this present life and not in hell. However, the sura is better read as a single story, where both husband and wife share in the same curse. So I prefer this interpretation:

4. That Abu Lahab's wife (as part of *his* curse, as well as hers) is forced to provide the firewood which is then used to burn and thus torment her husband. In this reading, then, the three verses that speak of burning can be connected. Abu Lahab (Father of Flames) is burned using wood provided by his wife.

Regarding the necklace of plaited palm-fibers, the *masad* of the title, nobody knows how it functions in the sura. There is no question about the meaning of the word, but it remains undetermined how *masad* is used in this context. In sura 40, men in hell have iron collars around their necks:

> when the iron collars will be placed in their necks and tied in chains they will be dragged. (Q 40:71)

This is from the book of Deuteronomy:

> Therefore you shall serve your enemies whom the LORD will send against you, in hunger and thirst, in nakedness and lack of everything. He will put an iron yoke on your neck until he has destroyed you. (Deut 28:48)

By inference, Abu Lahab's wife, because she is a woman, has a similar, though gentler, collar around her neck.[7] However, the sura itself does not support this idea that the collar is a lenient hellish punishment.

The sura takes its name, Surat-al-Masad, from this final image. The names of the suras usually employ an unusual or prominent word for the title as an identifying feature. These titles do not always represent the most important feature of the sura. They usually do, however. This is what the early readers of the sura imply by giving it this name. The name, Surat-al-Masad, focuses the reader's attention: A woman with a rough-woven straw collar is burdened under a weight of kindling. Her labor brings her low and humiliates her. If she is in hell delivering the firewood that burns her husband, the necklace, then is a collar like a dog's, that forces her to do it. The fire burns (or will burn) her husband. The three words for fire intensify the suffering:

He will *burn* in a *fire* of *flame*. (Q 111:3; my trans. and italics)

Plainly, someone (it does not say who) is torturing or will torture the unhappy couple.

THE IDENTITY OF ABU LAHAB

The influential medieval commentaries often recount stories from the ancient biographies and the Hadith as a lens by which to correctly interpret the sura. These ancient sources explain obscure verses of the Qur'an. Many such stories coalesce around sura 111, Surat-al-Masad. These stories, "occasions for descent," or "occasions of revelation" ('asbāb al-Nazūl) explain the exact historical context in which the sura was revealed to the Prophet.[8] Every one of these early sources identifies Abu Lahab as one of Muhammad's uncles. This uncle opposed his nephew's prophecies. These sources give him the name Abdul Uzza. The name Abdul Uzza has a meaning too. It means, "slave of Uzza." Uzza is the name of one of the three goddesses, God's daughters, that the Arab tribes worshiped at the time of Mohammad. Another sura mentions these goddesses (see Chapter 2):

---

7 An internet comment I read suggested "she is 'enjoying' the leniency in the Hell-Prison being a lady." This is an unattributed quote from an Islamic website called *Discover True Islam* (http://www.free-minds.org). Another comment reads, "She is one of the worst woman criminals, yet unlike men who will have iron yokes, she being woman is treated comparatively softly." See the following link for these two quotes: http://free-minds.org/forum/index.php?topic=9601005.0/.

8. I go into more detail on 'asbāb al-Nazūl in the Introduction.

Have you seen [considered] al-Lat, and al-Uzza, and Manat the
third, the other . . . God has not sent down any authority for it. . .
They only follow conjecture. (Q 53:19–20, 23)

Abdul Uzza was Uzza's priest, and Uzza's image resided in the Ka'ba,
along with the images of other Arabian gods and goddesses. In medieval
Islamic lore, Abdul Uzza serves as a Judas-like figure to Muslims, a villain
who hated Muhammad. Other members of the Prophet's tribe might have
hated Muhammad, not only because the Prophet disparaged their gods,
but also because he hurt Meccan businesses. Their trade depended upon
the regular pilgrimages to the Ka'ba. In contrast, Abu Lahab opposed the
Prophet because of Abu Lahab's loyalty to Arabian polytheism. He hated
Muhammad's monotheistic teachings. It was not about the money.

In these later traditions, portraits of three different figures merge. First
is Abu Lahab (the main subject of Surat-al-Masad, the one who will burn in
hell). Second is the uncle of the Prophet (who opposed the Prophet's teaching). And third is Abdul Uzza (the priest of the goddess Al-Uzza). He serves
the goddess in the Ka'ba. Of those three, the Sura knows only of its princi-
pal subject, Abu Lahab, who will burn. The earliest sources connecting the
figure of Abu Lahab to the Prophet's uncle and to the priest of Uzza come
two centuries after the death of Muhammad. Hisham Ibn Al-Kalbi wrote
The Book of Idols, in which he links Abu Lahab and Abdul Uzza. However,
he does not call Abu Lahab the uncle of the Prophet. In a second volume,
one that includes a detailed genealogy of the Prophet's family, the Prophet's
uncle Abdul Uzza (a relatively common name) is connected with Abu Lahab in parentheses.[9] This constitutes the very first connection between the
three figures in extant texts.

In the stories that begin to cluster around sura 111 in the Middle Ages,
these three figures (quasi-distinct from each other) combine in different
ways. The relationship between Abu Lahab and Muhammad becomes a key
feature of this emerging narrative. Whereas the sura itself does not specify
the reason for Abu Lahab's punishment, the later traditions add details about
his many violations. They accuse him of ignoring tribal obligations when he
did not protect his nephew Muhammad from persecution. This offense is
implied by tribal patterns of family and clan loyalty. They expect Muhammad's uncles to support their nephew. The other two uncles, Abu Talib and
Hamza, both supported and protected the Prophet. Abu Lahab's transgression is also theological in that he opposed monotheism and Muhammad's

---

9. I am reading this work in German and cannot reliably attest that the parentheti-
cal in some form is indeed in the original Arabic.

message. However, one can glean none of this information about Abu Lahab from reading sura 111.

These developing stories pile on detail after detail that heighten the opposition between Muhammad and Abu Lahab. In one tale, Abu Lahab's sons have married Muhammad's daughters. Abu Lahab orders them to divorce the women because of their association with the Prophet. In another story, Muhammad summons the members of his tribe, the Quraysh, to a meeting. He tells them that the tribe faces a dire threat, but he refuses to reveal the nature of the threat until they have all assembled. When they have gathered, he proclaims to the group the dangers of polytheism and condemns the worship of their old gods. He threatens them with hellfire. Abu Lahab feels manipulated (justifiably so, in my opinion) and directs an expletive toward the Prophet: He declares to Muhammad, *taban leka* (literally, "may you perish"). "Damn you!" would be the English equivalent.

The sura takes Abu Lahab's epithet, *taban leka*, and turns it back on himself. Using the same verb, the sura begins, *tabit yada Abi Lahab*, ("may the hands of Abu Lahab be destroyed" (Q 111:2). In other words, Abu Lahab says *taban leka* to the Prophet, and the petitioner prays that God will say, "I'll *taban* you!"

In another tale, Abu Lahab follows his nephew Muhammad to a different city. When Muhammad begins to preach, Abu Lahab publicly proclaims him a liar. He throws stones at Muhammad when he tries to address the crowd. We read that Abu Lahab's hapless wife, the one who carries fire to her husband's torture, once places thorns in Muhammad's path so that he cuts his feet when he walks by. It is at this point that Mohammad publicly recites Abu Lahab's curse, Q 111. The man's wife is incensed at the slander against her family, and she goes to see the Prophet to rebuke him. When she comes to the Prophet's home, God makes Muhammad invisible. The woman cannot find him and thus has no place to vent her anger. She leaves unsated.

These stories go far beyond what the sura says. However, most of the traditional Islamic interpretations of this sura depend upon these post-Qur'anic, extra-Qur'anic stories to give the verses meaning. The sura says nothing about Abu Lahab's opposition to Muhammad. It only says that Abu Lahab is wealthy and that his property will not help him:

> His wealth and what he has earned were of no use to him.
> (Q 111:2)

He has reason to expect that his possessions will smooth the way in his life and the next. Additionally, the sura describes him as a married man. None of the additional, clarifying stories find support or attestation in the sura itself. I do not disparage these traditional interpretations, nor do I mean to suggest that Abu Lahab is *not* Abdul Uzza, the Prophet's uncle. But to make those claims about Abu Lahab's identity, one must be privy to more information than what one finds in the sura.

INTERPRETATIONS OF THE SURA

When one uses these accompanying, parallel stories, the occasions of revelation, a single compelling narrative emerges. This narrative becomes the *meaning* of the sura for subsequent communities. I here paraphrase and re-tell the story of the sura as it emerged among early Islamic interpreters.

> After Muhammad had long endured his uncle's taunts and physical opposition, God gave vent to Muhammad's frustration by revealing to him Surat-al-Masad. One cannot know who exactly utters the curse, God or Muhammad. If it is God who curses, then God intends to punish Muhammad's uncle for opposing the Prophet. Alternatively, this curse comprises words that God gives for the Prophet to use. In that case, God bestows on Muhammad a powerful cursing formula by which he can damage his enemy. If the Prophet recites this incantation of destruction against Abu Lahab, he will thwart his uncle's efforts to oppose Islam. The sura, then, is the script of the curse that he sends against his uncle.

It is possible to read the sura without recourse to these accompanying stories. There were Muslims who did so, before these biographical materials became widely circulated. The sura would then have been understood as a general curse against those who are wealthy and complacent, those who believe their wealth will preserve them.[10] The second verse, "What good will his prosperity do him?" further suggests a cautionary tale about the danger of trusting in one's wealth. The book of James in the New Testament expresses a similar sentiment:

> Come now, you rich people, weep and wail for the miseries that are coming to you. Your riches have rotted, and your clothes are moth-eaten. Your gold and silver have rusted, and their rust will be evidence against you, and it will eat your flesh like fire. (Jas 5:1–3)

Notice the linked themes of riches and burning.

10. See Chapter 9 for another example of a complacent rich person.

THE HORROR OF THE SURA

Muslims regard this sura and the other brief ones at the end of the Qur'an as children's suras because they are short and easy to memorize. Even more, they appeal to children because they each create a single, powerful image, emotionally resonant and didactic, with simplistic divisions of people into the good and the evil.[11] However, the Surat-al-Masad is not exactly child-friendly material. It gives an account of the torture of two human beings as a punishment for their sins.

I compare this sura to the imprecatory psalms in the Hebrew Bible. These psalms wish unimaginable ill upon the heads of *their* enemies. In Psalm 137 for instance, the Temple Singer, dragged into exile, declares concerning infants born to his captors,

> O daughter Babylon, you devastator! . . .
> Happy shall they be who take your little ones
>   and dash them against the rock! (Ps 137:8–9)

Elisha the prophet cursed a group of children "in the name of the LORD [Yahweh]":[12]

> When he turned round and saw them, he cursed them in the
> name of the LORD. Then two she-bears came out of the woods
> and mauled forty-two of the boys. (2 Kgs 2:24)

This violent desire, this *religious* desire, to wish terrible harm on one's enemies certainly visits both sacred traditions, the Hebrew Bible and the Qur'an. The sura-speaker wishes an awful torment, a torture, upon this figure of Abu Lahab, wishing him burned to death with a triple fire.

> He will *burn* in a *fire* of *flame*. (Q 111:3; my trans. and italics)

This suffering troubles me. Abu Lahab's torture does not necessarily bring release or satisfaction because it is in poor taste, even immoral, to revel in the torture of others. However, the poet regards the torture of Abu Lahab as a *good* thing. There are only two ways that the human spirit can tolerate such violent wishing against a fellow human being. Either one believes that the human being has done something so heinous that only the greatest imaginable amount of pain and suffering is sufficient to restore balance and the moral equilibrium to the universe. Or, second, the sufferer must be regarded as less than human, a monster, vermin, only worthy of extermination. How then do we account for the hatred the sura expresses?

11. Chapter 1 examines the last two suras.

12. See my treatment of this story in Penchansky, *What Rough Beast?*, chapter 6.

Psalm 137 explains the source of such hatred. For instance the psalm expresses the pain of the refugee:

> How could we sing the Lord's song
>   in a foreign land?
> If I forget you, O Jerusalem,
>   let my right hand wither! . . .
> Happy shall they be who take your little ones
>   and dash them against the rock! (Ps 137:4–5, 9)

The poet, the one who wishes to crack open the heads of Babylonian infants, was torn from his home and forced to live in exile, powerless and dejected. Some such losses might be so grievous that they call up such violent wishing, and this verbal violence might (in itself) have a purgative effect or even bring healing. In Abu Lahab's curse, words such as these in the sura give voice to the pain that the early Islamic community felt at the violent opposition against them, inflicted by family and neighbors. This sura would then function as a means of empowering the embattled Islamic community in their early suffering. The sura's glee at the torment of Abu Lahab is a result of the sufferings of the early Muslims. Abu Lahab becomes a potent symbol to focus the sense of hatred and powerlessness. It predates the later stories about Muhammad's uncle. The sufferings of Abu Lahab and his unnamed wife provide an imaginary balance to the Muslims' present grievance.

In the Bible, the prophet Nahum gives voice to God, who sings for joy at the destruction of the Assyrians:

> I will throw filth at you
>   and treat you with contempt,
>   and make you a spectacle.
> Then all who see you will shrink from you and say,
>   "Nineveh is devastated." (Nah 3:6–7)

John of Patmos sings a victory song over Babylon the Great:

> Hallelujah, for her smoke rises forever. (Rev 19:3)

The psalmist takes joy in having a "perfect hatred" toward his enemies (Ps 139:22). The matriarch Miriam leads the rescued Israelite slaves in a chorus, celebrating the mass death of the Egyptian army by drowning:

> Sing to the LORD, for he has triumphed gloriously;
>   horse and rider he has thrown into the sea. (Exod 15:1)

This is in a sense a *psychological* interpretation: The sura is offered as a means by which to vent violent emotions, and by giving them voice (but not acting upon them or truly wishing them) to achieve healing. I want to offer a different interpretation—a *theological* interpretation that sees the hatred as a *bad thing*. Unfortunately, the joy in the destruction of one's enemies, the delight in seeing them suffer, is a pervasive religious sentiment. This we acknowledge, and then do our best to quench the fires that give it destructive force. Surat-al-Masad is born of hatred and a desire for revenge, to see one's enemy suffer, and to see one's enemy's wife humiliated and enslaved. The speaker resents Abu Lahab's success and for that reason delights in seeing that his wealth and his increase will do him no good. This deep-seated tendency to wish ill on others comes from a bleak and destructive place in the human psyche.

Does anyone deserve the terrible punishment wished upon Abu Lahab? Is it proportional to his imagined sins? Does God enforce such terrible curses? Why is it that we tend to exonerate behavior from God that we would not, should not, accept from any fellow human being? When will we cry out along with the great patriarch Abraham,

Shall not the judge of all the earth do what is just? (Gen 18:25)[13]

---

13. We will revisit this passage in Chapter 5.

Surat-al-Kahf Q 18:60–82
The First Story

(Remember) when Moses said to his young man, "I shall not give up until I reach the junction of the two seas, or (else) I shall go on for a long time." When they reached the junction of them, they forgot their fish, (for) it had taken its way into the sea, swimming off. So when they had passed beyond (that place), he said to his young man, "Bring us our morning meal. We have indeed become weary from this journey of ours." He said, "Did you see when we took refuge at the rock? Surely I forgot the fish— none other than Satan made me forget to remember it—and it took its way into the sea—an amazing thing!" He said, "That is what we were seeking!" So they returned, retracing their footsteps.

The Second Story
Moses Meets the Stranger

And they found a servant, one of Our servants to whom We had given mercy from Us, and whom We had taught knowledge from Us. Moses said to him, "Shall I follow you on (the condition) that you teach me some of what you have been taught (of) right (knowledge)?" He said, "Surely you will not be able (to have) patience with me. How could you have patience for what you cannot encompass in (your) awareness of it?" He said, "You will find me, if God pleases, patient, and I shall not disobey you in any command." He said, "If you follow (me), do not ask me about anything, until I mention it to you."

Three Incidents on the Road

So they both set out (and continued on) until, when they sailed in the ship, he made a hole in it. He said, "Have you made a hole in it in order to drown its passengers? You have indeed done a dreadful thing!" He said, "Did I not say, 'Surely you will not be able (to have) patience with me?'" He said, "Do not take me to task for what I forgot, and do not burden me (with) hardship in my affair." So they both set out (and continued on) until, when they met a young boy, he killed him. He said, "Have you killed an innocent person, other than (in retaliation) for a person? Certainly you have done a terrible thing!" He said, "Did I not say to you, 'Surely you will not be able (to have) patience with me?'" He said, "If I ask you about anything after this, do not keep me as a companion. You have had enough excuses from me." So they both set out (and continued on) until, when they came to the people of a town, they asked its people for food, but they refused to offer them hospitality. They both found in it a wall on the verge of collapse, and he set it up. He said, "If you had wished, you could indeed have taken a reward for that."

The Explanation

He said, "This is the parting between me and you. (Now) I shall inform you about the interpretation of what you were not able (to have) patience with. As for the ship, it belonged to poor people working on the sea, and I wanted to damage it, (because) behind them (there) was a king seizing every ship by force.

As for the young boy, his parents were believers, and we feared that he would burden them both (with) insolent transgression and disbelief. We wanted their Lord to give to them both in exchange (one) better than him in purity, and closer (to them) in affection. As for the wall, it belonged to two orphan boys in the city, and underneath it was a treasure belonging to them both, (for) their father had been a righteous man. Your Lord wanted them both to reach their maturity, and bring forth their treasure as a mercy from your Lord. I did not do it on my (own) command. That is the interpretation (of) what you were not able (to have) patience with."

5

Surat-al-Kahf (The Cave Sura)

Q 18:60–82—Moses and the Stranger[1]

Texts in comparison: Genesis 2:10–14; Genesis 18;
Psalm 73; Job; Wisdom of Solomon 4:10–14

If Surat-al-Masad in the previous chapter causes the reader to question divine judgment against the wicked, this sura, the Cave Sura, compels readers to question God's treatment of the innocent. Sura 18 contains two connected stories whose protagonist is Moses.[2] The first story gives an account of Moses and his servant on a quest to find the fabled junction of the two seas. In the second, Moses becomes disciple of a mysterious, God-imbued Stranger.

THE FIRST STORY

The story begins when Moses introduces his quest:

---

1. An earlier version of this chapter appeared as "A Qur'anic Theodicy," in Sirry, ed., *New Trends in Qur'anic Studies*, 95–108.

2. Many have noted how little Moses in this sura has to do with the Moses who led Israel both in the Bible and in the Qur'an. "Newby identifies three different 'Mosesses' in the comments reported to have been collected by Ibn Ishaq" (Wheeler, "The Jewish Origins," 155).

> I shall not give up until I reach the junction of the two seas, or
> (else) I shall go on for a long time. (Q 18:60)

This "junction of the two seas" represents an in-between place, where heaven and earth meet. Wheeler observes, "Moses' quest for the meeting place of the two waters [is] a journey to the water of life flowing out of the Garden of Eden at the ends of the earth."[3]

Anything can happen in such a place. However, Moses and his slave had failed to notice that they had in fact reached the junction. Rather, blind in their ignorance, they continue on past it without stopping. Although they had reached their destination point, they remain oblivious to its sacred character. Additionally, while at the sacred place, the narrator writes,

> they forgot their fish, (for) it had taken its way into the sea, swimming off. (Q 18:61)

Moses, later in their journey, asks his slave to prepare their meal. Presumably, Moses expects that they will eat the fish they have brought. Then the slave confesses his loss:

> Did you see when we took refuge at the rock? Surely I forgot the fish. (Q 18:63a)[4]

The slave blames Satan for making him forget the fish, or perhaps for making him neglect to tell Moses that they had lost their meal:

> None other than Satan made me forget to remember it. (Q 18:63b)

He figures Moses would never believe that their lunch just rose up and swam away. The slave describes the fish's behavior using the same words the narrator had used in v. 61:

> it took its way in the sea. (18:63c)

and adds a final comment:

> . . . an amazing thing! (Q 18:63d)

It was certainly a marvel for a dead fish to revive and swim away. From this, Moses discerns where he might find the junction of the two seas. He

---

3. Wheeler, "The Jewish Origins," 170.

4. When he says, "We took shelter at the rock," he is further corroborating that they did not know they were at the junction, or he would have described the place differently.

identifies it by its life-giving power. When Moses hears this, instead of scolding the slave for losing their breakfast, as the slave fears, Moses declares,

> That is what we were seeking! (Q 18:64)

They leave their meal and break camp to retrace their steps.

> The resurrection of the fish when it touched the water of life . . .
> [was] intended as a sign to Moses that he had reached the meeting place of the two waters.[5]

WATERS OF LIFE IN THE BIBLE
AND CHRISTIAN TRADITION

In the Bible too one finds life-giving waters in pictures of paradise. In Genesis, a primeval river flows and divides into the four great rivers of creation:

> A river flows out of Eden to water the garden, and from there it divides and becomes four branches. The name of the first is Pishon; it is the one that flows around the whole land of Havilah. . .
> The name of the second river is Gihon; it is the one that flows around the whole land of Cush. The name of the third river is Tigris, which flows east of Assyria. And the fourth river is the Euphrates. (Gen 2:10–14)

The book of Ezekiel describes a river flowing out from the four corners of the restored temple:

> Then he brought me back to the entrance of the temple. There water was flowing from below the threshold of the temple. (Ezek 47:1)

Ezekiel goes on to describe the healing qualities of the water, which would certainly have power to revive a dead fish.

> When it enters the sea . . . of stagnant waters, the water will become fresh. Wherever the river goes, every living creature that swarms will live . . . everything will live where the river goes. (Ezek 47:8–9)

There is a remarkable affinity between Ezekiel's account of the life-giving water that flows from the temple and the Qur'anic account of the

---

5. Wheeler, "The Jewish Origins," 163.

life-giving water at the junction of the two seas. They both bring back to life what was dead.

There are stories similar to this Qur'anic account, roughly contemporary to the sura, in postbiblical Christian traditions. In these tales, Alexander the Great is the protagonist who seeks the magical waters and subsequently witnesses a dead fish brought back to life. There are Jewish tales as well, with similar plots. In these, the prophet Elijah is protagonist. These parallel narratives give clarity concerning the true purpose of Moses's quest in the sura. Moses wants to find the waters of life, because they will bring youth and immortality to those who immerse themselves.

The story in the Qur'an does not reveal what happens next. Rather, it ends abruptly. The reader does not learn what transpires when Moses and his slave return to the fabled place. As it stands, the story leaves the reader stranded. However, this is the first of two stories about Moses, stitched together in this sura. This first story lacks an ending, which leaves the reader restless, craving some resolution. This desire for closure causes her to search for a continuation of the first story in the second. Therefore, this relatively brief account (Q 18:60–64) attaches itself to the second story (Q 18:65–82), which is much longer. For Bukhari (810–870) they are not two stories but rather one, which he explains by providing a smooth and detailed narrative. In Bukhari's version, God tells Moses that he will find what he seeks in the place where he loses his fish.[6]

But let us first read the passage itself without these embellishments. Immediately, at the conclusion of the fish story, the reader faces a new narrative with the same named protagonist as the first, Moses. This second narrative lacks a beginning. Most readers (as Bukhari does) will naturally seek to combine the two. As the reader continues beyond the first story, she desires closure. One does not find a concrete connection between the stories other than the repetition of the name Moses. This in condensed form is Bukhari's narrative: Moses searches for the junction between the two seas. There he finds the Stranger, the main protagonist of the second story.

The Qur'an calls this stranger "one of Our slaves" (Q 18:65). Early post-Qur'anic commentaries call him Khaḍir, the Arabic word for "green." Schwartzbaum observes, "Even the earliest Moslem exegesis identified this unnamed 'abd [slave] with the "Green Prophet," Khaḍir or Khiḍr. The earliest Islamic records containing this identification date back to the end of the first century of the Hijra [the seventh century BCE]."[7]

---

6. Schwarzbaum, "The Jewish and Moslem Versions," 132, 149–50.
7. Schwarzbaum, "The Jewish and Moslem Versions," 132.

This connection between the two stories tightens because the second story begins abruptly: Moses meets

> one of [God's] slaves. (Q 18:65; my trans.)

I call him the Stranger to distinguish him from Moses's slave in the first story and to emphasize his mysterious identity. It is a small leap of inference to assume that Moses meets this Stranger at the junction between the seas, and that what Moses is seeking there is not the waters of life as in the first story, but rather this Stranger. As mentioned earlier, when there are gaps or ambiguities in a Qur'anic text, later interpreters replace the gaps with stories. These stories explain the ambiguities and fill in the missing places. In this case, the early interpreters add a scene, a prequel, to the first story. This narrative portrays Moses as a rabbi gathered with his students. When lecturing to them, he brags that he is the wisest human on earth. After Moses makes such a grandiose statement, God, to teach him humility, sends him on a quest to find someone wiser than himself:

> Moses rises to address the Children of Israel and someone asks him who is the most learned among them. When Moses answers that he himself is, God reveals that one yet more learned awaits Moses at the confluence of the two seas.[8]

THE SECOND STORY

As mentioned above, the ambiguous transition between the two stories leads the reader to combine them, to read them as one. However, to do that, one must fill in narrative gaps with invention. At the end of his quest, at the junction of the two seas, Moses meets the Stranger. In the reader's mind, Moses's quest for the water of life has transformed into a quest to gain wisdom from this Stranger. Although these two stories *may* be read as a single work, the two Moses narratives originated as two distinct stories with significantly divergent narrative arcs.

Nevertheless, the second story, consisting of seventeen verses, swallows up the first story, which only contains four verses. Whatever function or meaning the first story may have had on its own, it now only serves to introduce the second. Originally, it might have been similar to earlier Jewish and Hellenistic stories, an account of the quest for the waters of eternal life. Now it serves to introduce Moses as a diligent seeker, and it places him in a magical place where unusual things are possible.

8. Renard, "Khaḍir/khiḍe," 81.

We learn no more about the fish or about the junction of the two seas. Even if the waters brought a dead fish to life, this is no longer what interests Moses. His slave from the first story makes a brief appearance when Moses embarks upon his second adventure. Moses and his slave encounter the Stranger, a figure first identified as "one of God's slaves" (Q 18:65). After this, Moses's slave disappears. This Stranger, we are told, has been blessed and taught by God. Moses then asks that the Stranger teach him the things God has taught him (Q 18:66). The Stranger discourages Moses's request:

> "Your mind," the Stranger says, "cannot possibly comprehend
> the mysteries of what God taught me." (Q 18:68; my trans.)

Moses swears that "if God wills," he will persevere and do whatever the Stranger commands:

> You will find me, if God pleases, patient, and I shall not disobey
> you in any command. (Q 18:69)

In response, the Stranger reluctantly agrees to allow Moses to accompany him. He lays down one condition upon which he will accept Moses as his student—Moses must not ask any questions.

> If you follow (me), do not ask me about anything, until I mention it to you. (Q 18:70)

Instead, Moses must await the Stranger's explanations whenever anything confuses him.

The narrative then recounts three incidents. Schwarzbaum calls them three "atrocities."[9] Each is introduced by the statement, "so they both set out until . . ."(see Q 18:71, 74, and 77). The incidents have in common that in each the Stranger does something inexplicable and disturbing, and in each case Moses breaks his silence, though silence had been the requirement of his discipleship.

In the first incident, they take passage on a boat. The Stranger sinks or attempts to sink the boat while they are on it.

> "What are you doing?" Moses cried. "Are you trying to drown us
> all?" (Q 18:71; my trans./para.)

The Stranger only responds,

> I told you that you were incapable of being patient with me.
> (Q 18:72; my trans.)

---

9. Schwarzbaum, "The Jewish and Moslem Versions," 133.

Moses begs for another chance:

> Do not take me to task for what I forgot, and do not burden me
> (with) hardship in my affair. (Q 18:73)

In his response, Moses takes a defensive and self-justifying tone with
the Stranger. He is not at all contrite. Even so, the Stranger accepts this half-
hearted apology, and they continue their journey. In the second incident,
they see coming towards them a young child. Without warning or provocation, the Stranger attacks and murders the child.

> So they both set out (and continued on) until, when they met a
> young boy, he killed him. (Q 18:74a)

The text offers none of the details. Does the Stranger pick up a stick
and club the child to death? Does he strangle the child? Throw him off a
cliff? The narrator allows the reader's imagination to visualize the scene.
Moses cannot look away from the horror he had just witnessed. He explodes
in rage:

> Have you killed an innocent person . . .? You have done a terrible
> thing! (Q 18:74)

The Stranger, unperturbed, repeats the same litany from before:

> I told you that you were incapable of being patient with me.
> (Q 18:75; my trans.)

Moses begs for another chance:

> If I ask you about anything after this, do not keep me as a com-
> panion. You have had enough excuses from me. (Q 18:76)

In this, his tone has changed considerably from what it was in v. 73, his
earlier apology. This time Moses is abject and repentant.

Off they go again. In the third incident, the pattern differs from the
other two. The set-up and explanation are much longer.[10] Moses and the
Stranger enter a village that refuses to receive them. The Stranger finds a
broken wall in the town and fixes it. Moses, incensed at this apparent generosity to the benefit of a selfish and inhospitable people, says,

---

10. The first event is fifteen words, the second is sixteen words, and the third is
twenty-three words. Regarding the explanations (discussed below), the first is eighteen
words, the second nineteen (in two verses)—v. 80 has ten words; v. 81 has nine words.
The third explanation (v. 82) has thirty-four words. This indicates that this third story
and its explanation are less sharply drawn and are structurally uncomfortable fitting in
with the other two stories.

At least you could have charged them. (Q 18:77; my trans.)

Moses has now questioned the Stranger a third time. In doing so, he has used up all his chances. The Stranger banishes him, finally and decisively:

This is the parting between me and you. (Q 18:78)

Before they part however, the Stranger explains each of the three behaviors that had so infuriated Moses. These explanations get to the heart of the story. Along with Moses, the reader has been eager to find out what motivated the Stranger to act in these ways. They seem inexplicable at best, indefensible at worst. What the Stranger says to justify his behavior produces the theological content of the narrative.

These are the explanations:

The Stranger informs Moses that the boat that he sank belonged to a family who depended upon it for their livelihood. He sank the boat because an evil king was about to advance on the community and confiscate all the boats. The Stranger made the boat unusable in order to prevent this evil king from taking it:

As for the ship, it belonged to poor people working on the sea, and I wanted to damage it, (because) behind them (there) was a king seizing every ship by force. (Q 18:79)

In regard to the second incident, the Stranger explains that he killed the child because he feared that the child would become a burden to his believing parents.

As for the young boy, his parents were believers, and we feared that he would burden them both (with) insolent transgression and disbelief. (Q 18:80)

According to Tabari (839–923):

This boy is described as exceedingly handsome, rich and lovely. His parents rejoiced when he was born and awfully grieved over his death. Had he remained alive he would have caused their annihilation.[11]

The Stranger explains that God will give them a better child:

We wanted their Lord to give to them both in exchange (one) better than him in purity, and closer (to them) in affection. (Q 18:81)

---

11. Quoted in Schwarzbaum, "The Jewish and Moslem Versions," 152–53.

Regarding the third incident, why did the Stranger fix the wall? He begins by explaining that a father had hidden a treasure in the wall to benefit his two sons. After the father died, the wall fell into disrepair. The Stranger repaired the wall so that the treasure would remain hidden until the brothers came of age.

As the Stranger leaves Moses, he spits out a parting insult:

> That is the interpretation (of) what you were not able (to have) patience with. (Q 18:82)

The Stranger is confirmed in his opinion that Moses is incapable of understanding God's mysteries.

The second story ends at this point.

THE MYSTERIOUS STRANGER AND GOD

The Stranger in the second story is an ambiguous figure who represents God. Later interpreters treat him as a quasi-divine being. In the sura he is unnamed. God has shown him divine mercy and has taught him divine knowledge.

> They found a servant, one of Our servants to whom We had given mercy from Us, and whom We had taught knowledge from Us. (Q 18:65)

He acts on God's behalf. On the most basic level, the Stranger claims divine mandate for each of his actions. The Stranger insists:

> I did not do it on my (own) command. (Q 18:82)

As further evidence of blurring between what the Stranger does and what God does, when the Stranger repairs the wall, the Qur'an describes the action as "a mercy from the Lord." When explaining why he killed the child, the Stranger speaks in the first-person plural ("we," "our," "us"), which is characteristic of divine speech. For example, the Stranger says,

> We feared that he would burden them both. (Q 18:80)

Compare this to the earlier verse:

> And they found a servant, one of *Our* servants to whom *We* had given mercy from *Us*, and whom *We* had taught knowledge from *Us*. (Q 18:65, italics added)

The blurring of God's and the Stranger's identities is not consistent.
Other parts of the Stranger's speech make a clear distinction between the
two. However, even there, what the Stranger does, he declares, is what the
Lord wants. Regarding the third incident—the repairing of the wall and the
brothers related to it—the Stranger says:

> Your Lord wanted them both to reach their maturity, and bring
> forth their treasure as a mercy from your Lord. (Q 18:82)

Sometimes the two variant ideas (that God and the Stranger are the
same and that God and the Stranger are distinct) combine in the same sentence as when the Stranger is quoted as saying,

> . . . we wanted that their Lord . . . (Q 18:82)

"*We* wanted," is God talking. "Their Lord" makes a distinction between the speaker and God. The Qur'an deliberately blurs the identities of
God and the Stranger.

If the Stranger stands for God in this Sura, then the Stranger's disturbing and inexplicable actions comment upon the times when God causes
disturbing and inexplicable events in life. When the Stranger explains his
actions, *that* explanation constitutes a defense of God's governance of the
universe. In other words, this narrative presents a theodicy. It represents a
Qur'anic understanding of the problem of evil and serves as a way to speak
about theologically sensitive subjects while keeping God at a distance, because God must never be challenged.

The Stranger's explanations (Q 18:79–82) assume that behind every
inexplicable event, whether inflicted disaster (the first two incidents in the
Sura) or the unexplained benevolence of the Stranger (the third), God has
hidden reasons. Schwarzbaum says it succinctly: "The Koranic notion of an
apparently unjust or queer act [is that] which turns out to be of benefit to
the righteous."[12]

If those involved in these three incidents had known the divine intention, they would have been able to make sense of the chaos and seeming
randomness of their lives. The Stranger, by which we mean God, sinks the
boat to thwart an evil king's designs. He kills the child as a mercy to the
parents. He hides the treasure to protect the two orphan brothers. Most
people do not know the divine plan. The family that owned the boat did not
know that an evil king was stealing boats. The parents could not have known
that their child would have grown into a monster. And the brothers could
not have known about the treasure, hidden for their own good. God has

12. Schwarzbaum, "The Jewish and Moslem Versions," 148.

secret intentions in each of those cases, carried out by the Stranger. Things happen that seem disastrous. From the viewpoint of those who suffer, these bad things that happen (the sinking of a boat or the murder of a child) are examples of evil entering the world. This is because the characters affected by these events lack the divine perspective. From God's perspective, the actions of the Stranger make perfect sense. The Stranger's explanations deign to give that perspective.

As a result, the Cave Sura can be understood as a defense of God's governance of the world. God has reasons, it says, not apparent from a human perspective. This is why the Stranger forbids Moses to ask any questions. There are some things beyond human perspective that must just be accepted. One must affirm divine goodness when the evidence points otherwise. The Stranger's explanations of why he did what he did show that God has reasons for everything that happens. However, because Moses could not possibly understand those reasons, he was supposed to be patient and not question. This story then becomes a model for the faithful when confronting tragedy.

Here is the crux. If we regard the story as an argument in favor of God's effective governance of the world and base it on the Stranger's admonitions to Moses and his explanations, then *they are very bad explanations.* Schwartzbaum agrees, saying, "The justification of the first two queer acts is rather of a trivial, unconvincing nature."[13]

In the first explanation, the Stranger, by sinking the boat does indeed prevent an evil king from appropriating it by force. However, that does not help the family that has lost the boat. Regarding the murdered child in the second story, would the pious parents be grateful that their son was murdered? Would they not rather have seen him alive? How could the Stranger think that the parents would be satisfied with exchanging an old child for a new and better one?

Each of these actions is horrible on its face. When the Stranger reveals the hidden reasons, these explanations are no less horrible than the actions themselves. According to Tha'labi (d. 1035), Moses ultimately regrets having chosen to meet such a nasty fellow, one who commits atrocities. Further, the Stranger only *fears* (Q 18:80) that the child will turn out badly. That he "feared" suggests that he is not sure how the child will turn out.

> The 'abd, [Arabic for "slave," the Qur'an's name for the Stranger]
> in this case of committing a heinous crime exhibits his gnosis,

13. Schwartzbaum, "The Jewish and Moslem Versions," 156. The account of the two orphans and the wall only loosely fits the schema, in that it represents the *benevolence* of God's unpredictable actions. Someone suggested to me that the Stranger's meddling actually prevented the brothers from obtaining the treasure, and therefore was not benevolent at all. I find that possible but not likely.

or rather his extraordinary prescience predicting the future depravity of the murdered boy. In other words, [he kills the child]
in order to save both the righteous parents and their still innocent son from the impending iniquity and apostasy which will
be brought about by the future evil deeds of the boy.[14]

Later commentators argue that *because* the young child dies before he
can be wicked, his death is a blessing to him as well as to his parents. The
book of Wisdom makes a similar assertion about the death of a youth:

> There were some who pleased God and were loved by him,
>   and while living among sinners were taken up.
> They were caught up so that evil might not change their
>   understanding
>   or guile deceive their souls . . .
> Being perfected in a short time,
>   they fulfilled long years;
> for their souls were pleasing to the Lord,
>   therefore he took them quickly from the midst of
>   wickedness. (Wis 4:10–14)

How do you suppose the parents feel about their son's death? The
Stranger's action on the boat is disturbing. The Stranger's murder of the
child is horrific.

According to the Stranger, God's ways, though mysterious and often
unknowable, are always good and favorably disposed towards human well-
being. This must be affirmed even when it might appear otherwise. In the
Bible, Psalm 37 expresses a similar sentiment:

> I have been young, and now am old,
>   yet I have not seen the righteous forsaken
>   or their children begging bread. (Ps 37:25)

My professor, James Crenshaw, calls this verse, "the Creed of the Willfully Blind." It is so obviously wrongheaded. It does not accord with how
humans live in the world. Rather, it sounds the voice of privilege and entitle-
ment, *blind* to the realities of pain and suffering. The Stranger's theodicy
insists that God's hidden ways intend good for the faithful subjects. The
Stranger's insistence that Moses not ask any questions and his explanation of
God's hidden reasons, assume that people are incapable of seeing the goodness and benevolence of God's actions in their suffering. That assumption is
"willfully blind." The Hebrew Bible offers two ways one might understand
God's hidden reasons for the world's pain:

14. Schwarzbaum, "The Jewish and Moslem Versions," 143.

1. Some monotheistic texts argue that one can never know or understand God's reasons, so one must trust and not ask questions.

2. Others assert that by asking questions and diligently searching for answers, one may gain access and understand God's hidden plans. These two ways emerge in the conflicting Israelite wisdom traditions in the Hebrew Bible.

The book of Proverbs says,

> Trust in the LORD with all your heart,
>   and do not rely on your own insight.
> In all your ways acknowledge him,
>   and he will make straight your paths. (Prov 3:5, 6)

This verse makes two points: First, it expresses trust in God's benevolent governance of the universe; and second, it insists that God's ways remain mysterious. One must not rely on human wisdom to find answers. This accords well with the claim of the Stranger in the sura, who has an explanation for every odd and tragic occurrence—an explanation available only to him and no other. He admonishes Moses not to ask questions but instead accept this basic claim that the universe is governed rightly and makes sense, but only if one has the whole picture. God's slave, the Stranger, has that whole picture. Moses does not. Therefore, one must "trust in the LORD" (Prov 3:5).

Moses provides an alternative understanding and response against the cruelty and randomness of the Stranger's behavior. He protests! Compare Moses's protest with the words of this psalm:

> Truly God is good to the upright,
>   to those who are pure in heart.
> But as for me, my feet had almost stumbled;
>   my steps had nearly slipped.
> For I was envious of the arrogant;
>   I saw the prosperity of the wicked . . .
> All in vain I have kept my heart clean
>   and washed my hands in innocence. (Ps 73:1–3, 13)

The psalmist rages against what appears a fundamental unfairness of how God treats the righteous. The bad people get all the breaks, while the psalmist and those who are pure in heart, trying to be good, suffer grievously. The psalmist despairs of his efforts to do right. What's the point of trying? He then transitions to a more trusting position:

> But when I thought how to understand this,
>   it seemed to me a wearisome task,

> until I went into the sanctuary of God;
>> then I perceived their end. (Ps 73:16–17)

The psalmist enters the temple, and there he finds God's presence. In that place he gets the overview that he lacked. *Now* he understands how the wicked will suffer in the end. The psalmist does not mean that the wicked will end in the afterlife where people receive their reward and punishment. Rather, the psalmist insists that *in this life* they will suffer for their sins. At the end of the poem, the psalmist reverts to the traditional view that God's ways appear correct to those who have knowledge.

In the temple, in God's presence, he finds that knowledge. However, as the fortunes of Israel change, the Israelite sages begin to challenge this notion. They respond to such happy endings by seriously questioning God's righteousness and raising doubts about God's goodness. For example, Job accuses God of attacking him like a wild animal:

> He has torn me in his wrath, and hated me;
>> he has gnashed his teeth at me;
>> my adversary sharpens his eyes against me. (Job 16:9)

The author of Ecclesiastes questions whether anything matters at all.[15]

> Vanity of vanities, says the Teacher,
>> vanity of vanities! All is vanity.
> What do people gain from all the toil
>> at which they toil under the sun? (Eccl 1:2–3)

The genius of the Hebrew Bible (one of them, anyway) is its ability to hold in tension absolutely opposed points of view. In this case, the traditional approach uncovers one side of the equation—the assertion that God, all wise and just, understands everything perfectly, and so it is futile and stupid to question anything that God does or says, as recorded in holy text. If God does it, it is good by definition. If God says it, it is true by definition. This seems so logical from a certain theological perspective. People who hold to this refuse to even consider the other side of the discussion. On the other hand, in Genesis, Abraham protests the injustice when he hears that God intends to destroy the righteous with the wicked. He declaims:

> Shall not the judge of all the earth do what is just? (Gen 18:25)

This implies that if God were to do this thing (destroy the righteous with the wicked), that would mean that God had behaved badly. That was

---

15. See Penchansky, *What Rough Beast?*; and Penchansky, *Understanding Hebrew Wisdom* for a full treatment of these issues.

Abraham's accusation. What was God's response? God *listened* to Abraham and changed plans as a result.

> [God] answered, "For the sake of ten I will not destroy it."
> (Gen 18:32)[16]

In a similar way, Moses in this sura protests against what appears to him random violence against innocent people:

> Have you killed an innocent person? . . . Certainly you have done a terrible thing. (Q 18:74)

That same injustice outrages Job:

> Know then that God has put me in the wrong,
>   and closed his net around me.
> Even when I cry out, "Violence!" I am not answered
>   I call aloud, but there is no justice.
> He has walled up my way so that I cannot pass,
>   and he has set darkness upon my paths. (Job 19:6–8)

Qoheleth, the author of Ecclesiastes, takes it further, questioning many of the verities of theism.

> For the fate of humans and the fate of animals is the same; as one dies, so dies the other. They all have the same breath, and humans have no advantage over the animals; for all is vanity. All go to one place; all are from the dust, and all turn to dust again. (Eccl 3:19–20)

Neither Job in the Bible nor Moses in this sura of the Qur'an dares go that far. They both however, along with Abraham in Genesis 18, question the fundamental claim of theism, that the God of revelation is good and can be trusted.

In sum, in the face of divine injustice, Moses cannot restrain himself. He complains loudly that the Stranger has acted immorally and foolishly. The two men part ways, but not before the Stranger explains his bizarre behavior. He sank the boat, he says, to keep it out of the hands of a rapacious king. He killed the child because he feared that it would grow up to be a crushing burden to his believing parents. He rebuilt the wall to protect a treasure buried there. Destroying the boat might keep it out of the king's hands but renders it useless to the poor family as well. Regarding the child, killing it because he fears that the child will turn out badly gives no comfort to the grieving parents.

16. In the end, God does destroy the Cities of the Plain. So it goes.

The Stranger's explanations for his actions are not credible. One might argue that the first readers would not have found the Stranger's explanations unreasonable. Perhaps the Stranger's impossible explanations did not trouble readers in the seventh century, and my objections to the Stranger's words are only the result of my modern sensibilities. On the contrary, doubts about the Stranger's behavior and his subsequent explanations are embedded in the text. Does the Qur'an intend the reader to take seriously these explanations or to question them? The Qur'an itself makes us interrogate the Stranger. Early commentators spent many words trying to justify the Stranger's explanations. This suggests that the Stranger's actions and words troubled them as well. What then might the sura mean when it offers for consideration explanations that readers are bound to question or at least feel uncomfortable about?

The key to understanding this sura and this tension is the Stranger himself. He serves as a cipher of God. On the most basic level, he claims that what he does he does at God's behest. The sura places him in a special category, as one of God's slaves. God bestows on him special portions of mercy and wisdom. But that will make him at most only a prophet. The sura deliberately blurs the identities of the Stranger and God. God acts through the Stranger, and on occasion speaks through him. Therefore, if the Stranger stands for God, and if the Stranger's explanations for his bizarre behavior are less than persuasive, this in fact produces a subtle and carefully nuanced theodicy. It weaves together two voices—alternative responses to suffering: a pious one represented by the Stranger, who urges trust, patience, and above all, *no* questions; and Moses's voice, though silenced at the end, protesting pointless pain and suffering inflicted on the innocent. Neither voice dominates, but both deserve to be heard.

Surat-al-Naml Q 27:15–44:
Solomon and the Ant

Certainly We gave David and Solomon knowledge, and they said, "Praise (be) to God, who has favored us over many of His believing servants!" Solomon inherited (it) from David, and said, "People! We have been taught the speech of birds, and we have been given (some) of everything. Surely this–it indeed is clear favor." Gathered before Solomon were his forces—jinn, and men, and birds—and they were arranged (in rows)—until, when they came upon the Wādī of the Ants, an ant said, "Ants! Enter your dwellings, or Solomon and his forces will crush you without realizing (it)." But he smiled, laughing at its words, and said, "My Lord, (so) dispose me that I may be thankful for your blessing with which You have blessed me and my parents, and that I may do righteousness (that) pleases You, and cause me to enter, by Your mercy, among your righteous servants."

Solomon and the Hudhud

He reviewed the birds, and said, "Why do I not see the hudhud? Or is it one of the absent? I shall indeed punish it severely, or slaughter it, or it will bring me a clear authority." But it did not stay (away) for long, and said, "I have encompassed what you have not encompassed, and I have brought you reliable news from (the people of) Sheba. Surely I found a woman ruling over them, and she has been given (some) of everything, and she has a great throne. I found her and her people prostrating themselves before the sun instead of God. Satan has made their deeds appear enticing to them, and he has kept them from the way, and they are not (rightly) guided. (He did this) so that they would not prostrate themselves before God, who brings forth what is hidden in the heavens and the earth. He knows what you hide and what you speak aloud. God—(there is) no god but Him, Lord of the great throne." He said, "We shall see whether you have spoken the truth or are one of the liars."

Solomon and the Queen of Sheba

"Go with this letter of mine, and cast it (down) to them. Then turn away from them and see what they return." She said, "Assembly! Surely an honorable letter has been cast (down) to me. Surely it is from Solomon, and surely it (reads): 'In the Name of God, the Merciful, the Compassionate. Do not exalt yourselves over me, but come to me in surrender.'" She said, "Assembly! Make a pronouncement to me about my affair. I do not decide any affair until you bear me witness." They said, "We are full of strength and full of harsh violence, but the affair (belongs) to you. See what you will command." She said, "Surely kings, when they enter a town, corrupt it, and make the upper class of its people the lowest, and that is what they will do. Surely I am going to send a gift to them, and see what the envoys bring back." When he came to Solomon, he said, "Would you increase me with wealth, when what God has given me is better than what He has given you? No! (It is) you (who) gloat over your own gift. Return to them! We shall indeed come upon them with forces which they have no power to face, and we shall indeed expel them from there in humiliation, and they will be disgraced."

The Test

He said, "Assembly! Which of you will bring me her throne before they come to me in surrender?" A crafty one of the jinn said, "I shall bring it to you before you (can) rise from your place. Surely I have strength for it (and am) trustworthy." One who had knowledge of the Book said, "I will bring it to you in the wink of an eye." So when he saw it set before him, he said, "This is from the favor of my Lord to test me (to see) whether I am thankful or ungrateful. Whoever is thankful is thankful only for his own good, and whoever is ungrateful—surely my Lord is wealthy, generous." He said, "Disguise her throne for her. We shall see whether she is (rightly) guided or is one of those who are not (rightly) guided." So when she came, it was said, "Is your throne like this?" She said, "It seems like it." And we had been given the knowledge before her, and were in surrender, but what she served, instead of God, kept her back. Surely she was from a disbelieving people. It was said to her, "Enter the palace." When she saw it, she thought it was a pool (of water), and she uncovered her legs. He said, "Surely it is a polished palace of crystal." She said, "My Lord, surely I have done myself evil. I surrender with Solomon to God, Lord of the worlds."

6

Surat-al-Naml (The Ant Sura)

Q 27:15–44—King Solomon and the Ant

Texts in comparison: 1 Kings 1–11 (especially 10:1–13);
Matthew 12:48–50; Luke 11:27–28; Luke 18:9–14

In the Ant Sura, the ant appears in only two verses (18 and 19) out of 93 verses total. It says,

> When they came upon the Wadi of the Ants, an ant said, "Ants! Enter your dwellings, or Solomon and his forces will crush you without realizing (it)." (Q 27:18)

Then in v. 19:

> But he [King Solomon] smiled, laughing at its [the ant's] words... (Q 27:19a)

Solomon's army marches through the Ant Valley. King Solomon in the Qur'anic narrative resembles, but not exactly, King Solomon featured in the book of 1 Kings in the Hebrew Bible (1 Kgs 1–11). In both the Bible and the Ant Sura, Solomon is a glorious and majestic king, and in both he has an encounter with the queen of Sheba. King Solomon has taken many forms in the Jewish, Christian, and Islamic traditions. Although King Solomon in *this* narrative has much in common with the same figure in 1 Kings 1–11 and the Chronicles (1 Chr 28, 29; 2 Chr 1–9), in some ways, he more resembles the figure of the king in the Song of Songs—powerful, dominating all he surveys. His royal procession in the Song of Songs finds echoes in a similar procession in the Ant Sura. This is the Song of Songs:

> What is that coming up from the wilderness,
>   like a column of smoke,
> perfumed with myrrh and frankincense,
>   with all the fragrant powders of the merchant?
> Look, it is the litter of Solomon!
> Around it are sixty mighty men
>   of the mighty men of Israel,
> all equipped with swords
>   and expert in war,
> each with his sword at his thigh
>   because of alarms by night. (Song 3:6–8)

This is from the Ant Sura:

> Gathered before Solomon were his forces—jinn and men, and birds—and they were arranged (in rows). (Q 27:17)

They march in front of Solomon in festal procession.

The Hebrew Bible depicts many facets of Solomon. The story of Solomon in 1 Kings might be described as a political romance. First Kings and 1 Chronicles depict Solomon as the wealthy and wise king whose weakness for women leads to idolatry and the erosion of his empire.

> For when Solomon was old, his wives turned away his heart after other gods; and his heart was not true to the LORD his God, as was the heart of his father David. (1 Kgs 11:4)

The book of Ecclesiastes depicts Solomon as a cynical king who has tried everything and finds it all empty. In the Wisdom of Solomon, he is the wise monarch. He collects gnomic sayings and epigrams in the book of Proverbs. The Ant Sura adds some new aspects to the tradition. It depicts Solomon as the leader of a vast supernatural army.

> Gathered before Solomon were his forces—jinn, and men, and birds . . . (Q 27:17)

Other suras speak of King Solomon's magical powers. He controls the wind. Demons and jinn must submit to him:

> And to Solomon (We subjected) the wind, blowing strongly at his command to the land which We have blessed . . . And among

the satans [the jinn—see Chapter 3], (there were) those who
dived for him and did other work besides. (Q 21:81–82)

And to Solomon (We subjected) the wind . . . and We made a
spring of molten brass to flow for him. And among the jinn,
(there were) those who worked for him by the permission of his
Lord. (Q 34:12–13)

So We subjected the wind to him to blow gently at his command, wherever he decided, and (also) the satans, every builder
and diver, and others (as well) bound in chains. (Q 38:34–40)

Back in the Ant Sura, while riding with this diverse army, Solomon hears
the ant's desperate warning:

Solomon and his forces will crush you! (Q 27:18)

It makes him smile. Then he breaks into laughter. He finds what the ant said
funny.

The story of Solomon and the ant occupies the center of the cluster
of stories in the Ant Sura. The names of suras were added at a later stage
in the Qur'an's formation, and sometimes they have scant relevance to the
main themes of the suras. Someone relatively early in the process of the
collection of Muhammad's revelations, saw this title as a convenient catch
phrase. The Ant Sura could well have been called (and with more space
given to these) the Moses Sura or the Solomon Sura. It could have been
named after the queen of Sheba, Lot, or the Arab prophet Salih. All of them
figure more prominently in the sura than the lowly ant. But they called it
the Ant Sura.

After vv. 1–6, the introduction, the sura recounts the story of Moses
(vv. 7–14). Moses sees a fire and hears God's voice. God gives him two signs
to show Pharaoh, but when Pharaoh sees the signs, he rejects them. The
Solomon narrative that follows is more complex, made up of three inter-
locked stories. The first I have already mentioned, the ant story. Solomon
and his army march into the valley of the ants. In the second, a hudhud
bird, one of Solomon's soldiers, brings a report to Solomon. He tells the king
about a queen whose subjects worship the sun. The third story showcases
Solomon's encounter with that queen. I will focus particularly on Solomon's
relationship with these three supporting characters—the ant, the hudhud,
and the queen of Sheba.[1] Each in their way comment on the unstable leader-

---

1. In Islamic tradition, her name is Bilqis. As much as I prefer to use names that sub-
vert the ancient patriarchal practice of not naming key female figures, in this case, *Bilqis*
represents much later traditions about the queen of Sheba, and so I will not use it here.

ship of the king. In the end, I will come back to the two verses about the ant, because they provide a key by which to understand the whole.

SOLOMON AND THE ANT

Solomon laughs at the plight of the ant. What does he do next? Muslim parents tell their children (and traditional commentaries concur) that Solomon turns his army away from the Ant Valley and thus he saves the tiny creatures from oblivion. One traditional story makes explicit what the Qur'an does not:

> Solomon smiled at the caution taken by the ants and ordered his hosts to await the ants getting into their holes and to be careful against causing any hurt to the ants in their passing over the land. [Solomon said] "How could my hosts hurt you and your kind as they are passing in air and do you not know that I am the prophet of God and would never act inequitably?"[2]

The story that emerges from early readers of the Qur'an comes to be told in such a way that it conforms to the belief that prophets could do no wrong. The sura however suggests the opposite. The Qur'an does not say whether or not Solomon tramples the ant city. However, the reader *desires* the ants to survive. The ants are sympathetic figures in this fable. Therefore, the reader decides whether or not the ants survive on the basis of how she feels about Solomon. If the reader believes in a flawless Solomon, then the king saves the ants. If Solomon is allowed flaws, then he crushes them. The Islamic tradition regards Solomon as a prophet and a righteous king of Israel who had extraordinary power and control over supernatural realms. Most importantly, they regard him as a Muslim, one who submitted to God. Therefore, he would never destroy the ant, an innocent, sympathetic figure.

Some ancient commentaries see Solomon's response of laughter as an expression of paternal affection and tenderness toward the ant. Such tenderness could only be inferred if one assumes beforehand a sensitive and attentive monarch. In spite of this long-standing interpretive tradition, the immediate context suggests that Solomon does in fact trample the ants. We can infer the character of Solomon from his behavior in the other two stories. In these stories, as we shall see, Solomon is an authoritarian bully. We therefore have reason to assume he would lack empathy toward the ants as well. Solomon's laughter suggests he does not take the threat to the ants seriously. The incident with the ant will be joined with two other acts of kingly violence. Another reason to see this as an ant massacre is that Solomon brags

2 Ali, *The Holy Qur'an Full Commentary*, 1147.

about how his family connections get him his great power and wealth, such that he would not care about a lowly ant. Solomon, indifferent to the fate of the ants, crushes them under the feet of his army and the hooves of his horses.

Solomon expresses amusement when he hears the ant's alarm.

> But he smiled, laughing at its words. (Q 27:19)

After he laughs, Solomon prays that God make him sufficiently grateful for all his manifold blessings. In Solomon's narcissism, the plight of the ants is forgotten.

> My Lord, (so) dispose me that I may be thankful for your blessing with which You have blessed me and my parents. (Q 27:19)

Apparently, the ants' plight reminds him how much God favors him and his family.

SOLOMON AND THE HUDHUD BIRD

Following the ant narrative, Solomon inspects his troops, which consist of jinn, humans, and birds. He finds that one of his soldiers, a bird, called in Arabic the hudhud, in English the hoopoe, is missing. Both names, hudhud and hoopoe, are efforts to reproduce the sound that the bird makes.

Solomon becomes enraged at the hudhud's absence.

> Why do I not see the hudhud? [he says.] Is he missing without authorization? I shall inflict harsh torture on him, or slaughter [him outright], unless he gives me a good reason for his absence. (Q 27:20–21; my trans.)[3]

We later learn of the hudhud's innocence. The hudhud explains his absence to Solomon. He was scouting unconquered territory to bring information back to the King. He was, in fact, not far distant at the time of Solomon's assembly. Even so, King Solomon intends to torture or execute this bird on impulse because he had failed to attend when the king had ordered his military into formation. This is Droge's translation:

> I shall indeed punish it [the hudhud] severely, or slaughter it . . . (Q 27:21)

---

3. Literally "punish him with a harsh punishment. Droge: "punish it [the hudhud] severely.

To explain his absence, the hudhud informs King Solomon he had spied on a queen who lives in a distant land. She leads a realm of sun worshipers. It is not clear which offends the bird more—the paganism of Sheba or the fact that her people are ruled by a woman.

> Surely I have found a woman ruling over them, and she has been given (some) of everything, and she has a great throne. (Q 27:23)

Solomon then sends the following letter to the queen:

> Do not exalt yourselves over me, but come to me in surrender. (Q 27:31)

The sentence literally says, "Come to me a muslim." The queen, however, suspects Solomon's intentions. In a council meeting, she says what she expects King Solomon to do:

> Surely kings, when they enter a town, destroy it, humiliate and debase all of the highborn people.[4] (Q 27:34; my trans.)

The queen tries to deflect the king by sending gifts, which he subsequently refuses. He accuses her of trying to make him appear needy:

> When [the queen's representative] came to Solomon, he said, "Would you increase me with wealth, when what God has given me is better than what He has given you? (It is) you (who) gloat over your own gift." (Q 27:36)

In contrast, the biblical account has Solomon accepting gifts from the queen,

> She came to Jerusalem with a very great retinue, with camels bearing spices, and very much gold, and precious stones. (1 Kgs 10:2)

In the Qur'an the king refuses those gifts and rejects the queen's delegation. In the Bible, Solomon seeks diplomatic relations; in Qur'an he seeks the queen's conversion. After the exchange between the monarchs, in a tirade, Solomon mirrors the queen's worst fears. He says,

---

4. Droge: "Surely kings, when they enter a town, corrupt it, and make the upper class of its people the lowest." The "humble classes" might have appreciated such a reversal. Because the sura depicts kings as rapacious, the royal family in Saudi Arabia discourages the reading of this sura in the mosques.

> We shall indeed come upon them with forces which they have
> no power to face, and we shall indeed expel them from there in
> humiliation and they will be disgraced. (Q 27:37)

"Humiliation" is the same word the queen uses in v. 34, and exactly the situation the queen had anticipated.

The gifts fail to placate Solomon. Rather, the king takes umbrage at the gesture because of his sense of superiority. He thinks it a paltry gift that would deign to add to Solomon's wealth. In the king's eyes, the queen has displayed arrogance to think she possessed anything he wanted or needed.

> Would you increase me with wealth, when what God has given
> me is better than what he has given you? (Q 27:36)

Later interpreters regard the queen's gift as an underhanded attempt to bribe Solomon away from his justice and piety. His anger, therefore, flows from a violation of his sense of honor. If one enters the narrative predisposed to a clean image of Solomon, one must continually make excuses and justifications for the king's irrational and violent outbursts against the queen and the hudhud. He threatens to crush the queen of Sheba on purpose as he crushed the ant by accident. When the queen tries to buy him off, he responds boastfully and arrogantly that he has more and better possessions than she.

Because Solomon rejects her gift, in a last, desperate effort to reduce tension between them, the queen personally visits Solomon at his palace. When she enters the royal grounds, the king administers two tests to determine if she is rightly guided.[5] He does this by testing the queen's ability in the fields of magic and artifice. The queen must see through the illusions placed before her by Solomon, and she must thereby determine the concealed reality behind them. In the first test, Solomon challenges her to recognize her own great throne, which Solomon has magically stolen from her and then disguised.

> When she sees the throne . . . it was said, "Is your throne like
> this?" She said, "it is as though it were the very same."[6] (Q 27:42;
> my trans.)

She proves herself rightly guided when she passes this first test by identifying the throne as hers. She refuses to fully commit herself, however.

---

5. "Guidance" is the Arabic word *huda*, a common Qur'anic term that refers to one's ability to know and follow God's correct path.

6. Droge: "When she sees the throne. . . it was said, 'Is your throne like this?' She said, 'It seems like it.'"

She admits that it *looks* like hers, but she shrewdly refuses to affirm its actual identity. She leaves the king hanging.

> It looks like it but might not be the same. (my trans./para. of
> Q 27:42)

The game is on as the two monarchs engage in a contest of wits. In the biblical text, these roles, the questioner and the one questioned, are reversed. The queen questions, and King Solomon proves his great wisdom by his answers:

> She came to test him with hard questions . . . Solomon answered
> all her questions; there was nothing hidden from the king that
> he could not explain to her. (1 Kgs 10:1, 3)

I do not understand how the first test, in which she recognizes her throne, informs Solomon whether or not the queen of Sheba is divinely guided. A rightly guided person is one who submits to God, that is, a Muslim. However, in the tests, Solomon only wants to prove that he can trick her, thus showing himself the wiser monarch. He hopes to humiliate her in the process. For the second test Solomon has constructed a smooth crystalline surface that creates the illusion of an expanse of water, a pool in front of the palace. In order to pass into the palace, the queen first must recognize the artifice. This time Solomon fools her. She uncovers her legs to wade in what she thinks is a large pool.[7] Solomon has fooled her into compromising her modesty by exposing her legs. Thus he humiliates her, as he had promised to do:

> We shall indeed come upon them with forces which they have
> no power to face, and we shall indeed expel them from there in
> humiliation, and they will be disgraced. (Q 27:37)

As a result of failing the second test, the queen of Sheba capitulates, submitting both to Solomon and to Solomon's God. She says,

> Lord, I have done myself evil. I surrender with Solomon to God,
> Lord of the universe. (Q 27:44)

Because of the aggression and implied threat in Solomon's earlier letter when he says,

> Come to me in surrender. (Q 27:31)

---

7. In the process of further demonizing the queen, a tradition emerged that when she exposed her legs, they were furred like an animal's, thus indicating that she was a demon (Lassner, "Bilqis," 229; Lassner, *Demonizing the Queen*, 88–132). Lassner sees this as an attack on uppity women.

when the queen submits and repudiates her previous worship, Solomon has won.

SUBMIT TO SOLOMON—SUBMIT TO GOD

When Solomon interacts with the queen, he uses some form of the word *muslim* to describe their relationship. The root of the word means "submission." It forms both the words *Muslim* and *Islam*. However, in the following instances, the meaning is ambiguous. In Solomon's letter to the queen, he writes:

> Do not exalt yourselves over me, but come to me in surrender (*muslimīn*). (Q 27:31)

When Solomon addresses the leaders in his army, he says:

> Assembly! Which of you will bring me her throne before they come to me in surrender (*muslimīn*)? (Q 27:38)

The speaker of this verse cannot be identified:

> And we had been given the knowledge before her, and were in surrender (*muslimīn*). (27:42)

This last verse, which also uses the word *muslim*, floats loose from any context, and might indeed anachronistically refer to Muslims as a distinct religious group.

In these contexts, the word may mean "submit to *God*," but submission to Solomon seems most likely. The fourth instance uses the verbal form *'aslamtu,* and, it *definitely* refers to God; the queen is speaking:

> Lord, I have done myself evil. I *surrender* [*'aslamtu*] with Solomon to God, Lord of the universe. (Q 27:44, italics added)

This verse that depicts the queen's submission is fraught with ambiguities. The queen opens the address by using the word *rab* ("lord") ostensibly addressing God,[8] but it was Solomon who had been speaking to her moments before. She might be calling *him* lord. She submits *with* Solomon. Admittedly, this could mean that she now regards Solomon as her elder brother in faith. More likely, however, she submits to Solomon's God, according to Solomon's express wishes. There is deliberate confusion or

---

8. The word *rab* ("Lord") functions similarly to *'adonāy* in Hebrew, and *kurios* in Greek. It is a word of address directed toward one who is a social superior and thus is used for human relations as well as for describing a human's relationship to God.

conflation of King Solomon and God in the passage. Therefore, I question whether Solomon and the queen stand together on one side, with God the only one who has power inhabiting the other side. Rather, Solomon is like God when he wielded power over the queen. He has brought low the great and independent queen by the threat of military force, by the failure of her peace initiatives, and finally by the king's two tests, the second of which succeeded in humiliating her. Both Solomon's power and his tests rob her of her confidence and her ability to rule. Even though I still find the tests ambiguous because they never make clear exactly what they show Solomon, they do result in her submission. She submits to the king and she submits to God. The two actions overlap. They might be the same.

THE CHARACTER OF THE QUEEN OF SHEBA

The queen of Sheba leads a nation of sun-worshiping people. The narrator says,

> But what she served kept her back. Surely she was from a disbe-
> lieving people. (Q 27:43)

In spite of this, she shows herself "rightly guided" when she recognizes her throne. She finally gives herself fully to Solomon's God after Solomon fools her with the glass sea. But even before the time when she becomes a Muslim in v. 44, the sura portrays her character as superior to the King's. The queen evokes the reader's sympathy in a similar way that the ant does earlier in the sura. The queen is the innocent victim of Solomon's effort to expand his territorial influence, whether his ambitions are spiritual or geopolitical.

When one looks at Solomon's flaws, it becomes easy to dislike the King. For example, Solomon thanks God that he is better than others. Regarding his inheritance, he and his father David say in unison,

> Praise (be) to God, who has favored us over many of His believ-
> ing servants! (Q 27:15)

For a second time, Solomon breaks out in prayer and thanksgiving, this time over the predicament of the ants. When he hears the ant's terrified cry, it causes him to pray to God that he be ever thankful that he is not the ant in her dire predicament. He does not care about the ants. Their plight causes him to gloat:

> My Lord, (so) dispose me that I may be thankful for your bless-
> ing with which You have blessed me and my parents. (Q 27:19)

Solomon, by these boastful prayers, challenges the basic Qur'anic idea that loyalty to tribal and family relations are *less* important than loyalty to the community of believers. For Solomon, all his blessings come by means of his blood relationship to David. In a counterexample, Noah, for instance, (in Q 11) welcomes into his boat those who believe. His son, an unbeliever, refuses to enter the ark and drowns. As a result, Noah is upset:

> And Noah called out to his Lord, and said, "My Lord, surely my son is one of my family."... [God] said, "Noah! Surely he is not one of your family." (Q 11:45–46)

Noah has to learn that the only ones who belong to his family are those who are righteous, not his blood relations. In a similar manner, Jesus in the Gospel of Matthew, when informed that his mother and relatives wish to see him, says,

> "Who is my mother, and who are my brothers?" And pointing to his disciples, he said, "Here are my mother and my brothers! For whoever does the will of my Father in heaven is my brother and sister and mother." (Matt 12:48–50)

In the Gospel of Luke, one encounters the same message:

> While he was saying this, a woman in the crowd raised her voice and said to him, "Blessed is the womb that bore you and the breasts that nursed you!" But he said, "Blessed rather are those who hear the word of God and obey it!" (Luke 11:27–28)

The Hebrew Bible (in Christian and Islamic caricature) portrays in part that covenant blessings pass down through family relations—from Abraham to Isaac, and from Isaac to Jacob, whose name is changed to Israel. Actually, the Hebrew Bible and the entire Jewish tradition emphasizes the importance of covenant faithfulness: belonging to the chosen line does not guarantee divine approval and blessing. Both Christianity and Islam have a greater emphasis that belief and right action trump tribal and family loyalties. In the sura, Solomon's boasts ill fit the Qur'anic ideal of equality. Solomon believes that God has blessed him *because* of his biological connection to his father David.

> Solomon inherited (it) from David, and said... it indeed is clear favor. (27:16)[9]

9. In an effort to defend the great King, some have suggested that Solomon in fact praises God for his *spiritual* blessings as opposed to his wealth. This is not accurate. Solomon evaluates what he possesses when compared to queen's paltry gifts. In a fascinating turn, this tension over inheritance becomes an occasion for a Shia-Sunni division. The

The king says in more than one place that God's blessings to him are better than God's blessings to others:

> Your blessings with which you blessed me and my parents.
> (Q 27:19)

Solomon's boastful prayers of superiority are negative omens. They suggest a way to interpret his behavior toward the queen, as well as toward the hudhud and the ant. Solomon is a self-absorbed, megalomaniacal leader. He is self-aggrandizing in two ways. First, because he claims that his prosperity comes through blood relations and not merit or faith. Second, because his boasting is predicated on how much more he has than anyone else.

> Praise (be) to God, who has favored us over many of His believ-
> ing servants! (Q 27:15)

He means others to marvel at how generously God has treated him. If he lived today, he would have gold fixtures in his bathrooms. Solomon believes that the blessing he received from God far exceeds what God has done for other righteous people.

He even acknowledges his theft of the queen's throne as a sign of divine generosity:

> This is from the favor of my Lord to test me (to see) whether I
> am thankful or ungrateful. Whoever is thankful is thankful only
> for his own good, and whoever is ungrateful—surely my Lord is
> wealthy, generous. (Q 27:40)

He bases all this thankfulness that he enjoys on his superiority to others. He sees his wealth as a test of his gratefulness. His thankfulness then is mixed with great fear that he might not be grateful enough. And further, Solomon feels the need to establish that he is wealthier than the queen, even though the sura in vv. 16 and 23 describes both of them as having been given "some of everything." Solomon says this to the queen:

> Would you increase me with wealth, when what God has given
> me is *better* than what He has given you? (Q 27:36, italics added).

Solomon threatens the independent state of Sheba, unprovoked, apparently for religious reasons, because the people of Sheba worship the sun. The hudhud had reported:

Shia believe that prophetic inspiration, rather than material blessings, passes through family ties from the Prophet through his family. The Sunni reject this biological succession of prophetic authority to members of Muhammad's family. They insist that the Prophet's inner circle, the Companions, inherited leadership of the community.

I found her and her people prostrating themselves before the
sun. (Q 27:24)

In contrast to King Solomon, the queen governs in a quasi-democratic
manner. When faced with King Solomon's letter and its demand to submit,
she consults with her officials:

Assembly! Make a pronouncement to me about my affair. I do
not decide any affair until you bear me witness. (Q 27:32)

Her military advisors, utterly devoted to her, are willing to go into
battle for her, and to submit to her authority. They say,

We are full of strength and full of harsh violence, but the affair
(belongs) to you. See what you will command. (Q 27:33)

In this respectful and formulaic exchange between the queen of Sheba
and her high council, she defers to their opinion and they to her. Such egali-
tarian leadership disturbs the hudhud. He expresses outrage that a woman
would rule over a peaceful land.

Later Islamic commentators accuse the queen of reversing the natural
order by ruling over men. However, she rules with equity and concern for
those under her authority. She is a careful diplomat and peacemaker. Solomon, in contrast, impulsive and unpredictable, throws a fit when he fails to
locate one of the birds in his army. He requires absolute, unswerving loyalty.
His army must cater to his slightest whims or shifts of mood.

THE ANT AND SOLOMON

There are two ways to view Solomon in the Ant Sura. In the first, Solomon,
a prophet of God and proto-Muslim, compels the sun-worshiping Shebans
and their queen to submit to God. From this perspective, the verses about
the ant earlier in the sura demonstrate the magnificence and magical powers of the great King. He leads a mighty army and understands the language
of animals.

We have been taught the speech of birds, and we have been
given (some) of everything. (Q 27:16)

Viewing Solomon from a different angle, one notices the King's negative qualities. He bullies the ant, the queen of Sheba, and the hudhud. He
ruthlessly forces less powerful nations to submit to his will. Before I move
on, I must consider a possible defense of Solomon's behavior. What seems
like boorish behavior to a modern reader might have seemed acceptable to

an ancient reader. That Solomon bullied animals and strong women might be what people expected of kings. However, the Qur'an dramatically portrays the contrast between the virtuous queen and the hotheaded and boastful Solomon. The author wants readers to *dislike* the great king.

There is however a third portrayal of Solomon embedded in the other two. Notice the following:

1. To submit to God is to be a Muslim. To submit to Solomon also means to be a muslim.

   When he writes to the queen, he says,

   > Do not exalt yourselves over me, but come to me in surrender (*muslimīn*). (Q 27:31)

2. Solomon sends a *kitʾab*, here in this verse translated "letter." The queen says:

   > Assembly! Surely an honorable letter [*kitʾab*] has been cast (down) to me. (Q 27:29)

   In the first verse of the sura, God too sends a *kitʾab* (here translated "book"):

   > These are the signs of the Qur'an and a clear book [*kitʾab*]. (Q 27:1)

   Kitʾab is another word for the Qur'an.

3. The queen reads this phrase at the beginning of Solomon's *kitʾab*:

   > Surely it is from Solomon, and surely it (reads): "In the Name of God, the Merciful, the Compassionate." (Q 27:30)

In God's *kitʾab*, the Qur'an, the suras always begins in this same way, with the bismillah.[10]

Thus, the depiction of Solomon in this sura and the depiction of God in the Qur'an overlap. The similarity is not a coincidence. Although many monarchs assume an air of divinity, that is not what I mean. The depiction of Solomon using these theological words represents a conscious effort by the author to evoke God. The keywords *kitʾab* and *muslim* and the words of the bismillah reveal the author's intention. The Solomon narrative, by

---

10. Many communications from Muslims begin this way, so it would not at all be unusual for the Muslim Solomon to so begin a letter. However, the cumulative evidence suggests that the statement alludes to the Qur'an as a *kitʾab*.

means of these verbal cues, becomes an indirect way for the sura to speak about God. Kings and landowners represent God in Jesus's parables.

> The kingdom of heaven may be compared to a king who wished to settle accounts with his slaves. (Matt 18:23)

> For the kingdom of heaven is like a landowner who went out early in the morning to hire laborers for his vineyard. (Matt 20:1)

In Jesus's parables from the Synoptic Gospels, as the examples above show, the connection between God and king, God and landowner, is made explicit. In the Qur'an the connection is less explicit and more subtle because of the Islamic aversion to comparing or associating God with anything else.

In the Hebrew Bible, the narrative of the prophet Micaiah ben Imlah (1 Kgs 22)[11] resembles this Solomon story. Briefly summarized, Micaiah recounts to the king how he listened in on a divine council. The council consisted of God (Yahweh) and beings identified as "spirits." Yahweh consults with the spirits to get their advice as to the most effective way that he might punish the king of Israel. What God does in 1 Kings 22, Solomon does in the Ant Sura. In both the sura and 1 Kings 22, a ruler receives counsel from a supernatural cohort, Yahweh as king in 1 Kings 22, and King Solomon in the Ant Sura. First Kings refers to the divine council in heaven. In the sura, Solomon leads a royal council. In both, the sovereign considers the fate of a world ruler, Jehoram in 1 Kings, and the queen of Sheba in the Ant Sura. The other members of the council (spirits in the Bible; jinn, birds, and humans in the Qur'an) act on behalf of the ruling monarch.

Solomon's story here serves as an indirect description of God. If the sura depicts Solomon negatively, what then does that say about God? The two verses in the sura that feature the ant address this question by analogy. Solomon stands for God, and his army represents the forces controlled by God. The story thus becomes a theodicy similar to the one found in the book of Job in the Hebrew Bible. The ant is a universal suffering figure, like Job.

This ant expects that Solomon and his armies will not even notice the devastation they inflict upon the ant village. She warns her kin:

> Ants! Enter your dwellings, or Solomon and his forces will crush you without realizing (it). (Q 27:18; my trans.)

---

11. I have referred to this unusual story from the Bible in four different chapters, (2, 3, 6, and 9). It is one of the few passages in the Bible that pulls back the curtain and lets us see the inner mechanism of prophecy.

However, Solomon does notice. He finds it amusing. What is the nature of that amusement? Mocking and condescending? Warm and affectionate? Does Solomon feel sadistic glee? Does he smash the ant city to be entertained? Or does he feel protective toward the ants? If one considers Solomon's subsequent behavior, his willingness to torture the hudhud and humiliate and dominate the queen of Sheba, one concludes that he feels no tenderness toward those weaker than him. The inhabitants of the ant city receive his disdain. Ancient readers sympathized with the ant. They quickly recognized the ant as the protagonist animal, a common figure in the fables. Further, ancient readers identified with the ants' plight. It was their plight as well—standing small and vulnerable in the face of large, destructive, exploitive powers they did not understand and could not control. Embedded in this text are traces of what the beleaguered Islamic community experienced in Mecca, crushed by the powers of the ruling Quraysh tribe.

The ant is a prophet who warns her people of impending destruction. However, note this important distinction. The prophets warn that God will take an active role in destroying the wicked. In the case of this ant, she warns of an impersonal force (as far as she is concerned) barreling down to destroy all her compatriots.

> Ants! Enter your dwellings, or Solomon and his forces will crush
> you without realizing (it). (Q 27:18)

Solomon laughs at the plight of the ants. He finds their life-and-death predicament (in their own homes, invaded by an alien force) amusing. The ant and her community suffer not because they have rejected God's "clear signs," as had Pharaoh earlier in the sura, but only because they are small and in the way. Solomon, divinely equipped to understand their plight, finds it laughable and an occasion to thank God for his own fortunate position when compared to theirs. In this, Solomon resembles the Pharisee in Jesus's parable:

> The Pharisee, standing by himself, was praying thus, "God, I
> thank you that I am not like other people: thieves, rogues, adul-
> terers, or even like this tax collector." (Luke 18:11)

In this parable, the Pharisee serves as a bad example, an example of what *not* to do.

Solomon's army will march across the valley of the ants and destroy them, not to punish them for their sins, but oblivious to their existence. Similarly, Job questions the reason for his great suffering, and God responds (I paraphrase), "You blame me for your suffering, but look at this universe

I'm running. What makes you think I pay any attention to you?"[12] Of course, in the book of Job, God is lying about his indifference to Job. In the prologue (chapters 1 and 2), God cannot stop talking about him. Twice he asks,

> Have you considered my servant Job? (Job 1:8, 2:3)

However, Solomon truly does not care about the ants.

Because the Qur'an regards King Solomon as a prophet, very quickly traditional interpreters regard him positively in spite of his actual depiction in this sura. Islamic interpreters refuse to accept Solomon as a flawed king. In a parallel development, these same commentaries demonize the figure of the queen of Sheba. Jewish and Christian interpreters do this as well, even though she is a relatively benign figure in both the Bible and the Qur'an. In both scriptures, she recognizes Solomon's superior wisdom and submits to it. In spite of this, the early Jewish commentaries on the Bible connect her with Lilith, who in Jewish tradition is the first wife of Adam. Lilith becomes the demonic killer of babies. All three traditions—Judaism, Christianity, and Islam—concoct stories about the queen's evil schemes. Therefore, when in the Qur'an she brings to the king her gifts, the early Muslim commentators interpret this as an opportunistic effort to bribe Solomon and turn him from his pious path. In medieval *tafsīr* (commentaries) she seduces Solomon, compelling him to marry her. One of their children becomes the notorious emperor Nebuchadnezzar, the Babylonian monarch who destroyed Jerusalem in the sixth century BCE.[13]

In the Qur'anic story, before the great king confronts the queen, he has the above-mentioned encounter with an outspoken ant. The ant passage is unique to this sura and has no parallels in other suras that mention Solomon. Nor does it appear anywhere in the Bible or in Jewish or Christian tradition.

The Ant Sura functions on a few different levels. The most obvious, of course, promulgates the message of *tawḥid* (monotheism), but this comes only at these points in the sura. The hudhud says:

> They would not prostrate themselves before God. (Q 27:25)

And he observes:

> God, (there is) no god but him. (Q 27:26)

Then at the conclusion of the narrative, the queen declares:

12. See my discussion of the book of Job in Penchansky, *The Betrayal of God*; and Penchansky, *Understanding Hebrew Wisdom*. This paraphrases Yahweh's argument in Job 38–41.

13. Solomon ruled in the tenth century BCE.

I surrender with Solomon to God, Lord of the worlds. (Q 27:44)

On another level, the use of animals, an ant and a bird, makes this story a fable, wherein animals stand in or represent various types of humans. A fable has its own rules of interpretation and its own linguistic codes that determine the reader's expectations. Animals in fables both teach wisdom and exemplify human foibles. In this case, the ant (and later the hudhud bird) suggest wisdom, in contrast to the figure of Solomon, whom the sura depicts as boorish, proud, and greedy. This description of the king is central to an understanding of the story.

At the ant narrative, the reader approaches a crossroads, a place where she must decide between multiple interpretations while not in possession of sufficient information: Does Solomon kill the ants or not? Here are two possible strategies by which one might navigate this crossroads. First, one might allow a particular theological position to control the reading. In the case of the Ant Sura, one would predetermine that Solomon, as a prophet and proto-Muslim, could not have been guilty of serious flaws. To believe that, one must filter out any contrary information. Therefore, Solomon saves the ants. The second way counterreads against the first. It examines the more immediate literary context—that is, the portrayal of Solomon elsewhere in the sura. Solomon projects a coherent personality throughout the three stories. At the interpretive crossroads, the fate of the ants is determined by considering Solomon's subsequent behavior toward those less powerful than him, both the hudhud and the queen.

Does Solomon turn his troops aside to avoid the valley of the ants? Running over the ants in the context of the story would constitute a bad and unsympathetic action. Subsequent traditions speak in great detail of how Solomon turned his troops aside to save the ants. However, the two stories joined to the ant narrative in the Sura (the accounts of the hudhud and the queen) each portray a Solomon who abuses a less powerful individual. If the Sura presents a consistent picture, then the reader would expect Solomon to abuse the ant community as well.

The ants, confronted with Solomon's indifferent army, face the terrifying universe. This crisis portrays the naked vulnerability of most peoples to the forces that remain outside their control. In the Ant Sura, like God, Solomon rules over a council of supernatural beings; like God, he sends his messengers with a *kit'ab*; and submitting to Solomon, like submitting to God, makes one a muslim. Both Solomon and God control great powers of destruction. The ant narrative then is a fable told about God and God's relation to people in their suffering.

The ant narrative portrays existence on the edge. The ants find themselves threatened by hostile and destructive forces, either unnoticed by God because of their size, or mocked by God who does not care. The sura holds that position in tension with another. It also presents a just God who rewards righteousness and punishes evil. This God provides clear signs embraced by believers. But we also see that God crushes humanity without awareness; or worse, that God, like Solomon, mocks the suffering of sentient beings. Together these two perspectives (Solomon the hero and Solomon the insecure despot) held in tension might bring one closer to understanding the story in its complexity. These verses constitute a sophisticated theodicy, able to maintain ambiguity and thus avoid the ever-present temptation to absolutism. The Ant Sura depicts Solomon and thus God as either unaware or vindictive. Job accuses God of a similar type of injustice. In the Job narrative, Yahweh, rather than rebuking Job for his arrogance, says regarding him,

> you have not spoken of me what is right, as my servant Job has.
> (Job 42:7)

By this final remark, God, and by extension, the author, affirm the correctness of Job's fearless accusations against God.

Likewise, the ant stands for those who suffer. Like Job's protestations, the ant's cry of danger and despair takes on a universal hue and becomes the strong, unanswered cry of the downtrodden.

Part 3

The Problem of Revelation

Jews, Christians, and Muslims believe their scriptures are revelation from God. The Qur'an claims to be an account of messages that the angel Gabriel brought in completed form to the Prophet Muhammad. These are word for word God's exact speech in the Arabic language. In Israel, the prophets were bearers of God's message to the people. They experienced the message themselves and proclaimed it. Subsequently, they or their disciples wrote their messages down for others.

However, both the Qur'an and the Bible are historical documents. They were written within particular historical contexts, and they reflect the interests and concerns of the people of that time. The Qur'an, for instance, refers to events that took place in seventh-century Arabia.[1] Israelite prophecy addresses its message first to its contemporary audiences.

This process gets more complex when a prophetic message recounts, refers to, or quotes, older stories, narratives known to the reader previously. In what way is that still revelation? In these cases, it becomes new revelation in the way the older story is used. The older story is transformed by its

---

1. See Chapter 4, Surat-al-Masad, an extreme example of historical-rootedness. It condemns an individual, likely a relative of Muhammad.

placement in this new context. In Chapter 7 I examine portions of the book of Hosea that provide a point of comparison with the story the Companions of the Cave. Both Hosea and the sura use older stories and older sources in their revelation, and they make something new out of them.

Sura 18, the Star Sura, describes two revelatory moments in the life of the Prophet Muhammad. In the first, a great and mighty figure appears to him, and in the second, the Prophet is transported to a mystical netherworld where he finds a magical tree. In that place, by that tree, a great sign appears to the Prophet. Both these incidents serve to authenticate the Prophet's message. They demonstrate that he did not fabricate the divine verses, and they make no doubt as to the divine source of these messages. In the Hebrew Bible, call narratives begin a prophet's career. Examples of call narratives in the Bible closely parallel Muhammad's two revelatory encounters. In a sense the Star Sura gives an account of the Prophet's call narrative. This is Chapter 8.

What about the one who bears the sacred message? How might a prophet distinguish the true God-sent message from the desires of the prophet's heart? And what is the relationship between the prophet's message and the prophet's life and moral character? Islam affirms that the Prophet Muhammad led an exemplary life, but the Qur'an reports lapses in his behavior. Chapter 9 addresses this topic. This final chapter considers what impact the character of the Prophet has on his prophetic message. Muhammad ignores a poor person who seeks spiritual help while at the same time he fawns over a wealthy and well-connected member of his community. An incident from the Gospels provides a useful companion to the Qur'anic story.

These three final chapters do not concern themselves primarily with the *content* of divine revelation but rather with the processes by which the revelation is conveyed through these singular individuals. The chapters demonstrate that the processes by which a prophet receives and conveys the message is more complex than a case of exact dictation of the divine message. The message is not unmediated, but rather has strong human features.

Surat-al-Kahf Q 18:9–25

Introduction

Or did you think that the companions of the cave and al-Raqīm were an amazing thing among Our signs?

(Remember) when the young men took refuge in the cave, and said, "Our Lord, grant us mercy from Yourself, and furnish the right (course) for us in our situation." So We sealed up their ears in the cave for a number of years, and then We raised them up (again), so that We might know which of the two actions would better count (the length of) time (they had) remained (there).

Take Refuge in the Cave

We shall recount to you their story in truth: Surely they were young men who believed in their Lord, and We increased them in guidance. We strengthened their hearts, when they stood up and said, "Our Lord is the Lord of the heavens and the earth. We do not call on any god other than Him. Certainly we would then have spoken an outrageous thing. These people of ours have taken gods other than Him. If only they would bring some clear authority concerning them! Who is more evil than the one who forges a lie against God?" When you have withdrawn from them and what they serve instead of God, take refuge in the cave.

In the Cave

Your Lord will display some of His mercy to you, and will furnish some relief for you in your situation. And you (would) see the sun when it rose, inclining from their cave toward the right, and when it set, passing them by on the left, while they were in the open part of it. That was one of the signs of God. Whoever God guides is the (rightly) guided one, and whoever He leads astray—you will not find for him an ally guiding (him). And you (would) think them awake, even though they were asleep, and We were turning them (now) to the right and (now) to the left, while their dog (lay) stretched out (with) its front paws at the door (of the cave). If you (had) observed them, you would indeed have turned away from them in flight, and indeed been filled (with) dread because of them.

The Companions Awake

So We raised them up (again) that they might ask questions among themselves. A speaker among them said, "How long have you remained (here)?" Some said, "We have (only) remained (here) a day, or part of a day." Others said, "Your Lord knows how long you have remained (here). So send one of you with this paper (money) of yours to the city, and let him see which (part) of it (has the) purest food, and let him bring you a supply of it. But let him be astute, and let no one realize (who) you (are). Surely they—if they become aware of you—they will stone you, or make you return to their creed, and then you will never prosper." So We caused (the people of the city) to stumble upon them, in order that they might know that the promise of God is true, and that the Hour—(there is) no doubt about it. When they argued among themselves about their situation, they said, "over them a building. Their Lord knows about them." Those who prevailed over their situation said, "We shall indeed take (to building) a place of worship over them."

The Controversy

Some say, "(There were) three, the fourth of them was their dog." But others say, "(There were) five, the sixth of them was their dog"—guessing about what is unknown. Still others say, "(There were) seven, the eighth of them was their dog." Say: "My Lord knows about their number. No one knows (about) them except a few." So do not dispute about them, except (on) an obvious point, and do not ask for a pronouncement about them from any of them. And do not say of anything, "Surely I am going to do that tomorrow, except (with the proviso): 'If God pleases.' And remember your Lord, when you forget, and say, 'It may be that my Lord will guide me to something nearer the right (way) than this.'" They remained in their cave for three hundred years and (some) add nine (more).

7

Surat-al-Kahf (The Cave Sura)

Q 18:9–25—Hosea and the Companions of the Cave

Texts in Comparison: Genesis 25–36;
Hosea 1–3, 12; 2 Kings 15–18

The message of a prophet sometimes takes over an older, well-known story, placing it in a new context and giving it a new meaning. By appropriating older material, a prophet connects the current audience with older streams of tradition, and the prophet's present message becomes infused a with greater authority and authenticity. In theory any two things can be compared. In practice, the compared objects must be sufficiently aligned so that one sheds light upon the other. The two prophetic narratives discussed in this chapter, one from the Qur'an and the other from the Bible, are similar enough so that they may be compared. From the Qur'an, "The Companions of the Cave,"[1] a section of sura 18, the Cave Sura, uses an older story. Netton calls its narrative "one of the most vivid in the entire Qur'an."[2] From the Hebrew Bible key parts of the book of Hosea may be compared to the sura. I compare them on three bases—first, their structure, second their uses of older stories, and third, their implied audiences. Hosea and the

---

1. Droge translates the word as "inhabitants," but the more widely used translation of the word is "Companions," which forms the common title of the group.

2. Netton, "Toward a Modern Tafsīr," 67.

Cave Sura incorporate these older stories in their prophetic message, stories familiar to their respective audiences.

There is a wide gulf between these passages from the Bible and the Qur'an that I must acknowledge. They differ geographically, chronologically, stylistically, and in their social location. Allowing for significant differences, they do in fact contain sufficient commonality so that one may create a space where the two shed light upon each other.

A QUICK OVERVIEW[3]

The book of Hosea divides neatly into two sections. The first, chapters 1–3, concerns the prophet's marriage to Gomer. God commands him to marry an *'šet zenûnîm*—"a wife of promiscuity."

> When the LORD first spoke through Hosea, the LORD said to Hosea, "Go, take for yourself a wife of whoredom and have children of whoredom, for the land commits great whoredom by forsaking the LORD." (Hos 1:2)[4]

The term *zenûnîm* is an unusual form, made from the common root *z-n-h*. The most neutral translation would be "promiscuity." God informs Hosea that she will bear "children of promiscuity" (*yeldêy zenûnîm*). This marriage and these children serve as an extended metaphor and object lesson. They demonstrate to the Israelites that the people of Israel worship other gods although married to the Israelite God, Yahweh. The definition of the phrase *'šet zenûnîm* remains controversial. The words do not clarify the exact nature of Gomer's transgression, and thus the use of this word throws open the text to multiple interpretations. Is she an unfaithful wife, or just *potentially* unfaithful wife? Is she a prostitute, a temple prostitute, or a priestess? All these have been claimed as the true understanding of Gomer. Was she promiscuous before the marriage, afterwards, or both?

The second part of Hosea, chapters 4–14, contain prophetic fragments of various lengths. Most reflect the political and military situation in eighth-century Israel, the Northern Kingdom, the same period one finds described in 2 Kings chapters 15–18. They portray chaos in the North, where a succession of kings is violently overthrown. At the same time, the country faces a looming threat from the Assyrian Empire. Ultimately, Assyria would overrun and conquer Israel and displace its population.

---

3. For a more detailed discussion of these issues, see Penchansky, "Hosea."

4. The NRSV and many others translate this word as "whoredom."

In the Qur'anic narrative called "Companions of the Cave," a group of monotheists rises in opposition against their polytheistic neighbors. They take a stand for the God of heaven and earth. God intervenes to protect them from persecution. He whisks them away, bringing them into a cave where he hides them and puts them to sleep for three centuries.

THE STRUCTURE

The first point of comparison between these passages in the Cave Sura and Hosea is their structure, or rather their lack of overall structure. Reading Hosea creates a tension within each of the two sections and between them. We see this first in the relationship of the first three chapters to one another. Chapters 1, 2 and 3 concern the prophet's marriage. Chapters 1 and 2 mention their children. Chapter 3 does not. The three chapters do not easily cohere. In the first chapter, the prophet marries, and his wife bears three children. It is written in the third person. Chapters 2 and 3 are written in the first person. Chapter 2 describes the prophet's divorce and subsequent reconciliation with his family. In chapter 3, the prophet describes his efforts to love and buy back a woman who has become enslaved to another man.

The three chapters can, with some effort, be read sequentially as three parts of the same story with the same characters. In chapter 1 they marry and have children. In chapter 2 they divorce. In chapter 3, after she becomes bound to another man, Hosea buys her back. Then he punishes her for her waywardness. However, the three chapters can also be read as concerning two women instead of one, or even as having to do with three different women. If we understand the text this way, Hosea had two wives in succession, Gomer in chapters 1 and 2, and an unnamed woman in chapter 3. I prefer reading these three chapters as each offering a different version of the same story, similar to the two creation stories in Genesis 1 and Genesis 2, or similar to the four Gospels, each of which retells roughly the same basic story.

In linking chapters 1–3 to the remaining chapters of Hosea, one notes first the significant differences between these two sections. They are different in genre and different in subject matter. Hosea chapters 1–3 are narrative. Hosea chapters 4–14 contain multiple genres, including oracle, narrative, and poetry. There is, however, linking the two sections the repeated use of different forms of the word *z-n-h*, which is used to describe Gomer and her children in the first section. Note how this word is used in an early poem in the second section:

> I will not punish your daughters when they play the whore
> [*tiznênah*—from the root *z-n-h*],

> nor your daughters-in-law when they commit adultery;
> for the men themselves go aside with whores [zonôt—from the
>   root z-n-h],
> and sacrifice with temple prostitutes [qedešôt]. (Hos 4:14)

Qedešôt literally means "holy women." It is the word for holy (qadôš) with the feminine plural ending.

Consider what this passage means. The prophet accuses the daughters of sexual indiscretion. They will not be punished, however, because their fathers do worse things. Specifically, their fathers have sex with prostitutes. It is the last phrase that has confounded exegetes—they "sacrifice with qedešôt." By linking these two words, zonôt and qedešôt, the prophet suggests a link between their cultic and sexual activity. It suggests that sexual misconduct took place between male worshipers and women.[5]

A closer examination of the relationship between the first section (chapters 1–3) and the second section (4–16) finds they are mostly very different. The first section is biographical while the second contains assorted prophesies. The two sections are not completely disconnected. Rather, the connection is troubled and difficult. Each section has a different style. They are connected by the word z-n-h and not by plot. That both sections are placed in this single defined book, the book of Hosea, compels the reader to read them together, as a whole.

One notes a similar complex structure in the Qura'nic "Companions" narrative. The story begins in the middle of a sentence. The first line is,

> Or did you think that the companions of the cave . . . were an
> amazing thing among Our signs? (Q 18:9)

The Arabic particle 'am (meaning "or") introduces a coordinating clause that should be preceded by a protasis, that is, an "either" clause, a first alternative, but there is none. Asad's translation adds this as a protasis:

> And since the life of the world is but a test, doest thou really
> think . . . (Q 18:9)

The other common translations either leave the phrase dangling[6] or drop the 'am altogether.[7] This invisible protasis, the initial clause, is implied but elusive. Is the unspoken alternate position that the miracle of the cave is

---

5. These are other places where qedešôt refers to cultic sexual activity: Gen 38:2; Deut 23:17–18; 1 Kgs 14:24, 15:12, 22:47, and 23:7.

6. See Droge, trans., The Qur'an; Pickthall, trans., The Glorious Koran.

7. See Sale, trans., The Koran; Nasr et al., eds., The Study Quran; and Dawood, trans., The Koran.

not a wondrous sign? Is it an ordinary sign or no sign at all? Who is it that takes this alternate position, whichever one that is?

In what follows, the Companions ask God for help to address a difficulty.

> Our Lord, grant us mercy from Yourself, and furnish the right (course) for us in our situation. (Q 18:10)

The "situation" they refer to is the opposition of the community to their monotheism. God takes them to a cave and puts them to sleep. After that, he awakens them. The text breaks off here. In the following verses, the story begins again, only this time in much more detail. The first line reintroduces the tale.

> We shall recount to you their story in truth. (Q 18:13)

The restarted tale begins differently than the first iteration. The Companions do not ask for help in this version, but rather, boldly take a stand for monotheism against their community.

> Our Lord is Lord of Heaven and Earth. [They say] We will not invoke any gods other than him. (Q 18:14)

After that, God hides the Companions in a cave.

> When you [the Companions] have withdrawn from them [the idolaters opposing them] and what they serve instead of God, take refuge in the cave. (Q 18:16)

The narrator describes their sleep in the cave in a scene both grotesque and frightening. God turns them over so they would seem awake to any chance observer.

> And you (would) think them awake, and even though they were asleep, and We were turning them (now) to the right and to the left. (Q 18:18)

The scene then begins to resemble a horror film:

> If you (had) observed them, you would indeed have turned away from them in flight, and indeed been filled (with) dread because of them. (Q 18:18)

Subsequently, when God awakens them, a voice (whether from God or one of their number is not clear) warns them to remain hidden and anonymous as they seek provisions for their company.

> But let him be cautious, and let no one realize (who) you (are).
> Surely they—if they become aware of you—they will stone you, or
> make you return to their creed, and then you will never prosper.
> (Q 18:19–20)[8]

The story ends abruptly there. The reader never finds out whether the
Companions are discovered, and what is their fate. This is another structural fault line. After some verses, the scene shifts years into the future when
unidentified people seek to preserve the memory of the Companions at the
site of the cave, which has become a shrine. They argue about whether or
not to build a structure, a *masjid*. *Masjid* is often translated "mosque." Here
it probably refers not to a formal mosque but to a simple place of prayer.
The structure is to be built over the cave, although teasing out the opposing
positions in this struggle is nearly impossible.

> When they argued among themselves about their situation, they
> said, "Build over them a building . . . We shall indeed take (to
> building) a place of worship [a *masjid*] over them." (Q 18:21)

How might we illuminate the points of disagreement? Is it between
those who want to build a shrine as opposed to those who are against
building anything? Are the shrine proponents against some *other* kind of
building? Is the building meant to be the tomb of the Companions? Is the
narrator *in favor* of the shrine or *against* it? Aisha, the Prophet's favored
wife, has been quoted as condemning those Muslims who revere the tombs
of sainted ancestors. She says:

> 'A'isha told of God's Messenger as saying in his illness from
> which he did not recover, "God curse the Jews and Christians!
> They have taken the graves of their prophets as mosques."[9]

Does the narrative of the Companions support Aisha's position or attack it? Just as in the first section, this part of the narrative also does not
resolve. The reader remains ignorant of the fate of the Companions. She sees
neither what was built over the site nor its purpose.

Next the narrator warns the reader against a certain unspecified
controversy.

> Do not argue with them [who *they* are is unspecified] unless
> you are certain. And do not ask them [that is, these unspeci-
> fied opponents] about them [that is, do not ask them about the
> Companions]. (Q 18:22; my trans.)

8. "You" is plural.

9. Bukhārī, *Sahih Al-Bukhari*, vol. 6, book 4, hadith 142.

My rendering of this verse (above) is a paraphrase.[10] The speaker here identifies two kinds of arguments that must be distinguished because they require different responses. First are arguments where the answer is obvious. The speaker here urges the listeners to pursue those kinds of arguments against their opponents. Second, there are less obvious arguments, which they must eschew. The speaker does not explain how one might tell the difference. Nevertheless, the sides are strongly polarized so that the narrator enjoins the reader not even to consult with the other side to gain information. Most interpreters identify these imagined interlocutors in the argument as Christians. Disputing about what? Perhaps they argue over exactly how long the Companions remained asleep in the cave. This was raised earlier in the sura:

> We raised them up (again), so that we might know which of the two factions would better count (the length of) time (they had) remained (there). (Q 18:12)

When awake, the Companions debated:

> Some said, "We have (only) remained (here) a day, or part of a day." Others said, "Your Lord knows how long you have remained (here)." (Q 18:19)

Later in the sura, the narrator seems to have settled the matter:

> They remained in the cave for three hundred years and (some) add nine[11] (more). (Q 18:25)

Finally, in the last verse of the narrative:

> Say: "God knows about how long they remained (there). To Him (belongs) the unseen of the heavens and the earth." (Q 18:26)

They might have argued over a different issue, found earlier in the sura:

> Some say "(There were) three, the fourth of them was their dog." But others say, "There were five, the sixth of them was their dog"—guessing about what is unknown. Still others say, "There were seven, the eighth of them was their dog." Say, "my Lord knows about their number." No one knows (about) them except a few. (Q 18:22)

---

10. Droge's translation is awkward: "So do not dispute about them, except (on) an obvious point, and do not ask (about) them except a few."

11. Probably allowing for the change between the solar and lunar calendars.

Some ancient commentaries argue that because the number seven appears after the "guessing" statement ("guessing what is unknown"), it is in
fact the correct number. But the final instruction is, "say, [only] my Lord
knows the number," an assertion repeated in the last verse of the narrative:

> Say: "God knows about how long they remained (there). To
> Him (belongs) the unseen of the heavens and the earth. How
> well He sees and hears!" (Q 18:26)

No one except God knows the correct answer to the controversy about
the number of inhabitants in the cave. This might be one of those arguments
the Qur'an warns against.

These controversies seem trivial to a contemporary reader, to me anyway. The number of years the Companions spent in the cave, give or take
a century, changes nothing of import in the story. Likewise, the number in
their company impacts none of the narrative's key elements. Neither are individual Companions specified so that a reader might ascertain their number. However, for some unknown reason these questions held great import
to the earliest readers. These admonitions concerning when and when not
to argue are not addressed to the Companions or to the builders of shrines
but rather to the first Muslims who are hearing or reading these texts and
who appear to engage in these controversies.

This sura narrative runs in fits, starts, and restarts, and does not read
as a smooth coherent story. The structure of Hosea is similar. This suggests a
few different ways these texts, both of them, were collected and transmitted.
They began as disconnected fragments strung together by topic. At some
point someone pasted them together with intimations toward a thematic
arrangement, but not much of one. That is one possibility. Another possibility is that someone chose to fashion this ambiguity, refusing to create
a single, unified narrative. In the act of reading, the reader tries to make
sense of what she reads or hears. When a narrative resists cohesion, it creates a sense of dissonance in the reader. It might cause her to reject what
is read. More likely, however, the reader experiencing this dissonance will
latch onto a single unifying idea and then ignore the parts that do not fit.
The story's dissonant features resist this effort, and that opens up the story to
multiple interpretations. Therefore, the structural deformities are smoothed
over with narration, or else ignored.

THE USE OF OLDER STORIES

This is the second way that I compare the Cave Sura to the book of Hosea. The "Companions" narrative retells an earlier story circulated among the Christian communities before the time of Muhammad. The Christian story is commonly known as "the Seven Sleepers of Ephesus." Its earliest version is found in the writings of a Syrian monk in the fifth century, Jacob of Sarug (c. 450–521) The story was very popular and had many versions in Western Christendom in the Middle Ages. Nwyia explains how such "borrowing" works in the Qur'an:

> When Muslim consciousness takes up for its own ends an event borrowed from the Bible or Judaeo-Christian hagiography, it in most cases cannot resist effecting a transvaluation by introducing fabulous details.[12]

This "transvaluation" is what is most important when assessing the Qur'anic and biblical use of older stories.

Hosea too transvalues older stories. For the sixth-century Judean editors who produced the book of Hosea, the narrative about Hosea's life as a legendary eighth-century prophet is already an old tradition. Also, the author or final editor of Hosea had access to ancient (from the author's perspective) stories of the Israelite kings, stories that subsequently found their way into the books of Kings. The king list in the introduction to the book (Hos 1:1) conforms to the order and names of the monarchs in 2 Kings chapters 14–17. Hosea 1:1 lists four Southern kings, Uzziah, Jotham, Ahaz, and Hezekiah, and one from the North, Jeroboam (known to scholars as Jeroboam II).[13] This king list represents one of the ways that Hosea used traditional Israelite histories. The story of the prophet Hosea and his family (Hos 1–3) constitutes a second layer of narrative. The story of Hosea's family is already an old story at the time of the book's formation. In Hosea, the existence of three loosely connected versions of the prophet's fractured marriage suggests that stories about this eighth-century prophet had been in circulation for a while. By the sixth century BCE, the time the book takes shape, Hosea is already a well-known figure.

The authors of the book of Hosea first use the older story about Hosea and his marriage (chapters 1–3). In chapter 12 one finds a different sort of old story. This chapter contains three brief references to the patriarch Jacob as found in Genesis. In the first mention, Jacob struggles in the womb

---

12. Quoted in Roberts, "A Parable of Blessing," 304.

13. The first Northern king named Jeroboam (tenth century BCE) split the nation away from King Rehoboam in 1 Kgs 12.

against his brother (Hos 12:3a; cf. Gen 25:26). In the second, Jacob wrestles with a divine figure, alternately called "God" and "the angel" (Hos 12:3b; cf. Gen 32:22–32). These details run in close parallel to the Genesis account. The author links these first two incidents, the babies in Rebekah's womb and Jacob wrestling with the angel, by making them parallel.

> In the womb he tried to supplant his brother,
>   in his manhood he strove with God. (Hos 12:3)

Jacob's contention with his fraternal twin somehow presages his later struggle against the divine.

The third incident mentions how Jacob works to earn the bride-price for Leah and Rachel.

> Jacob fled to the land of Aram;
>   there Israel served for a wife,
>   and for a wife he guarded sheep. (Hos 12:12)

This verse, Hos 12:12 (Jacob in Aram), is disconnected from the other two Jacob references, and would be out of order if the three had been arranged chronologically. In Genesis it occurs prior to his wrestling match with the angel.

The author of Hosea moves freely between Jacob referring to the patriarch of Genesis, and Jacob as an alternate term for the nation of Israel. For instance,

> The LORD has an indictment against Judah,
>   and will punish Jacob according to his ways. (Hos 12:2)

Jacob here is used to refer to the nation. The name Jacob reverts to referring to the person in the following quote:

> In the womb he tried to supplant his brother. (Hos 12:2)

One would expect that these references to Jacob in the book of Hosea comment upon the religious, political, or international situation of the nation or state of Israel, as does much of the prophetic material in Hos 4–14. However, these Jacob narratives do not in any way reflect the chaos in eighth-century Israel described elsewhere in Hosea and 2 Kings. The Jacob allusions only work in the context of Hosea if one assumes that *the entire story* of Jacob is known to the audience. Then the three allusions become reference points meant to evoke the whole.

When the sura uses the older Christian story "the Seven Sleepers of Ephesus," that known story underlies "the Companions of the Cave" in a similar way. The narratives, the ones found in Hosea and in the

"Companions," both assume that the reader has familiarity with an older story prior to reading about it in the Qur'an or the Bible. In both Hosea and in the sura, the omissions and changes to the original stories provide a key to understand their placements and functions in their current settings. For instance, Hosea adds weeping to the story of Jacob and the angel:

> He strove with the angel and prevailed,
>   he wept and sought his favor. (Hos 12:4)

The Genesis account contains no weeping. Either the Hosea author had access to some lost local tradition about Jacob, or else (as I suspect) the Hosea author added the detail for poetic effect. The weeping heightens and focuses Jacob's desperate need for the mysterious figure's blessing. It provides some further dimension to the complex character portrayed in the Genesis account.

We must not forget that the author of Hosea did not have access to the same account now known as Genesis 25–50. Editors put the book of Genesis in its present form at a time subsequent to the final formulation of Hosea in the sixth century. The writer of Hosea must have had access to an *earlier* version of the Jacob story that might or might not resemble the Jacob narrative in the book of Genesis. It would be important to know whether this earlier story emphasizes the negative or positive aspects of Jacob's career. Not knowing this makes it difficult for us to nail down the Jacob references in Hosea.

In the Jacob story in Genesis, Jacob has both positive and negative qualities. Jacob is a trickster who overcomes his difficulties through stealth and deceit, proving himself cleverer than his opponents. He deceives his brother, Esau, his father, Isaac, and his uncle, Laban. Jacob as trickster is viewed positively. From a negative perspective, those same encounters prove Jacob deceitful and predatory in his dealings with others.

When Hosea refers to Jacob, the author means to make an indirect comment about the nation of Israel. This is because as part of the Jacob story in Genesis Jacob's name is changed to Israel:

> You shall no longer be called Jacob, but Israel, for you have striv-
> en with God and with humans, and have prevailed. (Gen 32:28)

Jacob is the eponymous ancestor of the Israelites, that is, the father of his people, and they carry his name, Israel. Jacob's twelve sons became the founding ancestors of the twelve tribes of Israel. Because the specific references within the book of Hosea to the three incidents in Jacob's life do not yield specific and unambiguous links to Israel's situation, when Hosea refers to Jacob, he means to recall the whole of the Jacob narrative. Therefore one cannot know exactly how Hosea is using the Jacob narrative—whether

Israel is dishonest in the same way that Jacob is and in desperate need of conversion, or whether Israel by means of God's choice and its innate determination will prevail over all competitors. Jacob the character embodies both qualities that the Hosea author found in the nation. The flawed character of Jacob embodies the deficiencies of Israelite society (its greed, its amorality, and its dishonesty). If Jacob's cleverness and determination were emphasized in the Hosea author's version, that would suggest instead a hopeful future for Israel. There are different parts of Hosea that fit either scenario.

The Cave Sura works similarly in that it assumes the reader knows the details of the larger story, "the Seven Sleepers of Ephesus." The author of the Cave Sura assumes the reader's familiarity with the older story, details not present in the sura itself. For example, when the Companions awaken, a speaker brings up the subject of money:

> Send one of you with this paper (money) of yours to the city.
> (Q 18:19)

The sura never again mentions money. However, the money is a key detail in the older Christian story. In that tale, when the townspeople notice that the money the sleepers had used to purchase provisions comes from an earlier era, they realize that the sleepers have come from the past.

The sura assumes the reader knows the details not found in the Qur'anic account. That brings us to the glaring omission of an ending. In the original story, "the Seven Sleepers of Ephesus," the townspeople inform the Sleepers that while they slept in the cave, the king and surrounding community had converted to Christianity. In the Christian story, the Sleepers find safety in this new era. By contrast, the sura narrative cuts off with the Companions in hiding, fearful of discovery. Danger lurks everywhere. A voice warns them,

> If they become aware of you—they will stone you, or make you
> return to their creed. (Q 18:20)

The sura makes other changes and additions to the earlier, well-known story. The Christian story does not speak about an argument over the site of the cave. There is no trace of this dispute in the original story. Also, the sura adds the unusual detail of a dog who accompanies the Companions to the cave and guards its entrance:[14]

---

14. The Companions' dog echoes the seeming superfluous dog in the book of Tobit. "The young man went out and the angel went with him; and the dog came out with him and went along with them" (Tob 6:1–2). "As they went on together . . . the dog went along behind them" (Tob 11:4).

... while their dog (lay) stretched out (with) its front paws at the door (of the cave). (Q 18:18)

The narrative regards the dog as a member of the company:

Some say "(There were) three, the fourth of them was their dog." But others say, "(There were) five, the sixth of them was their dog"—guessing about what is unknown. Still others say, "There were) seven, the eighth of them was their dog." (Q 18:22)

THE SURA'S AUDIENCE

The audience of the Cave Sura is the early Islamic community. They would have been familiar with the basic elements of the original story of the "Seven Sleepers of Ephesus." Did the Islamic audience know the happy ending in the Christian story? Why then does the Qur'an leave it out? Perhaps the Qur'an's audience knew the ending, so there was no need to mention it. I think rather that the Muslim author excised the happy ending deliberately. This edited narrative as it now stands in the Cave Sura leaves the Companions in a world of danger and persecution. The truncated ending reflects the precarious situation faced by the small group of Muhammad's followers at the time they lived in Mecca.

As mentioned earlier, the sura gives specific instruction to the community about how to engage in debates, and when to avoid useless arguments. The admonition occurs in Q 18:22, which primarily concerns the exact number of Companions. The first Muslims would have been fully involved already in controversies over the details of the story, before they received this directive from the Prophet. They argued about how long the Companions slept, and what the number was of their company. We cannot know which side the Muslims took in these disputes, but they had strong opinions on both these matters that differed from the views of others who told of the story of the cave differently.

The audience for the prophesies of legendary Hosea (as opposed to the audience for the *book* of Hosea) is the aristocracy of eighth-century Israel—the royal families, the members of the priesthood, and the wealthy elite. The book imagines them listening to Hosea prophesy. The imagined author of the work (as opposed to the *actual* author) is the eighth-century prophet himself, introduced in the first verse.

The word of the LORD that came to Hosea, son of Beeri. (Hos 1:1)

The *actual* authors were a group of sages in sixth-century Judah. Their audience (the ones who read the book of Hosea) would have been their fellow sages and the wider Israelite audience in the sixth century BCE.

The expected audience for the Cave Sura and Hosea is most definitely *not us,* that is, contemporary readers. Both Hosea and the sura withhold key information, or else they left out information not readily available to a contemporary reader. As a result, the not-so-ideal reader must consult external narratives where available as a means to fill in the gaps in the ancient narrative. In the case of the sura, that means one must depend upon the previously written "the Seven Sleepers of Ephesus." Second Kings 14:23—20:21 and 2 Chronicles 26–28 provide the historical milieu for reading Hosea as a whole, and Genesis provides the backdrop for the Jacob references in chapter 12. In Hosea there are additional references to earlier events that had been mentioned in other parts of the Hebrew Bible. The towns of Admah and Zeboiim are mentioned in Hos 11. They are obscure references to the destruction of the cities of the plain in Genesis 18. God destroys Admah and Zeboiim along with their better-known neighbors Sodom and Gomorrah in Genesis 14:2. Also, Hosea often brings up the Israelite experience in the wilderness (Hos 7:13; 11:1; 12:3, 9; 13:4).[15]

The occasion of revelation (*'asbāb al-nazūl*) does not offer much help in the interpretation of these verses in the Cave Sura. It describes how a delegation from the Jewish tribes challenge Muhammad to recount the story of the "Companions of the Cave," which he does not know. The Prophet confidently says that he will bring the answer to their inquiry the next day. However, to his embarrassment, he has to wait thirty days before God will reveal to him the information now contained in the Cave Sura. After that humbling delay, he receives the words that became all or part of the Cave Sura.

Hosea and the sura each contain a complex, incomplete narrative, and in fact, narratives within narratives. In the sura, the narrative of the "Companions of the Cave" shows a group of young men shielded from persecution—hidden in a cave and put to sleep for three centuries. That narrative is subsumed into a story about a group who keeps alive the memory of the Companions through the construction of a shrine. That narrative in turn is subsumed by the commentary of the Prophet, who in recounting the shrine story weighs in on some of the controversies that have engaged the Islamic community about the proper way to interpret the story of the Companions. The book of Hosea follows a similar trajectory. It begins with

---

15. "Hewn by the prophets" (Hos 6:5) might refer to 1 Samuel, when Samuel "hewed Agag to pieces" (1 Sam 15:33).

the eighth-century prophet, whose name is mentioned only once, in Hosea 1:1. Hosea then becomes a character in the story of his marriage, thrice told in chapters 1–3. In the latter half of the book, the prophet himself becomes a storyteller, recounting key parts of the legendary tale of Jacob in chapter 12. And the whole book becomes a story in the hands of anonymous Judean tradents in the sixth century.

This comparison between Hosea and the Cave Sura affirms that both texts function similarly and are formed similarly. These authors wrote in fragments, held in many versions, put together and made uniform in subsequent generations. Both were directed to audiences that shared some knowledge of an earlier story, and so in both cases, the actual verses contain lacunae that must be filled in (or not filled in, as the case may be) by the reader. Both the story of the "Companions of the Cave" and the book of Hosea have a broken structure. The broken structure in Hosea is the difficult and troublesome merging of the first section (chapters 1–3) and the second section, (chapters 4–14) The structural break in the Cave Sura occurs first in the double beginning. Then the shift between three layered stories—the first, about the Companions; the second, an argument about what to build over the cave as a shrine; and the third, an argument between Christians and Muslims about the details of the first story.

The book of Hosea and this narrative in the Cave Sura, by judicious use of allusions to older stories, both draw in the reader while at the same time excluding her because she lacks key details that would make sense of the whole. The two works pull together incompletely linked pieces that suggest the lines of a story, but that ultimately do not fully cohere. The most common strategy for understanding these stories has been to impose an overall structure and then to ignore or harmonize the details that do not fit. Interpreters using this approach then fill in gaps in the narrative using external sources. I suggest an alternative strategy that does not seek to harmonize the disparate but rather to highlight and examine these tensions, as they are the sources of meaning.

Revelation in both these cases is more complicated than a simple transaction in which a heavenly messenger hands over a message to a prophet who then proclaims that same message verbatim to an audience. Rather, certain stories, well-known and widely disseminated, became subsumed in a prophetic envelope that connects the revelation to older cultural memories and transforms the story by addition and subtraction of details.

Surat-al-Najm Q 53:1–18:[16]

In the Name of God, the Merciful, the Compassionate.

The First Story Q 53:1–12

By the star when it falls! Your companion has not gone astray, nor has he erred, nor does he speak on a whim. It is nothing but an inspiration inspired [or "revelation revealed"—dp]. One harsh in power [or "mighty in power"—dp] has taught him. One full of strength, he stood poised, While He was at the highest horizon, Then He drew near and came down. He was two bow-lengths tall [or "two bow-lengths distant"—dp] And so he inspired his servant [or "slave"—dp] (with) what he inspired [or "revealed what he revealed"—dp]. His heart did not lie about what it [or "he"—dp] saw. Will you dispute with him about what he saw?

The Second Story Q 53:13–18

Certainly he saw Him at a second descent, By the Lote Tree of the Boundary, Near which is the Garden of the Refuge, When (there) covered the Lote Tree what covered (it). His sight did not turn aside, nor did it transgress. Certainly he saw one of the greatest signs [or "some of the greatest signs"—dp] of his Lord.

16. For ease of reference, I will refer to Q 53:1–12 as the First Story and Q 53:13–18 as the Second Story.

8

Surat-al-Najm (The Star Sura)

Q 53:1–18—By the Lote Tree

Texts in comparison: Exodus 3; 33; 34; Isaiah 6

The relationship between a prophet and God is fraught with ambiguity. How do they make contact? Is their communication mediated by an angel? Does the prophet encounter God directly? How does the prophet describe God? In antiquity, descriptions of deity fell between two extremes. At one extreme (for instance, in Homer's *Iliad*), the gods and goddesses are human-shaped deities, immortal, with great power, but prone to human foibles such as jealousy, favoritism, and violence. At the other extreme, the God of philosophy possesses every virtue in infinite quantity. God is all good, all-powerful, all knowing, everywhere present, outside of time. The Star Sura narrates two theophanies, moments when an apparition comes to Muhammad as part of his prophetic initiation. I compare these two connected Qur'anic stories to three similar prophetic divine encounters in the Hebrew Bible. Exodus chapters 3 and 33 and Isaiah 6 share common features with Surat-al-Najm. However, they all use different strategies to situate themselves somewhere between these two extremes of God as a human-shaped deity and God as a universal cosmic force.

The two stories in the Star Sura resemble what in the Hebrew Bible are known as call narratives. In each of these five texts (the stories in the Star Sura, two from Exodus, and one from Isaiah), a prophet is ushered into the divine presence. In each the reader is invited to witness the prophet's investiture, his initiation into the sacred mysteries. What distinguishes these stories from other call narratives[1] is how after promising so much, they refuse the reader access to the divine encounter at the center of each account. I will address three ways these texts obscure the divine presence. First, the author uses ambiguous language. Second, the prophet's view of God is hidden by an actual, physical covering. Third, the prophet creates confusion regarding the identity of the one who brings the revelation.

OBSCURING LANGUAGE

The First Story from Surat-al-Najm

Later Islamic tradition connects the first of these two stories in Surat-al-Najm to Muhammad's first revelation in the cave of Hirah. The second story is linked to the Prophet's night journey to heaven—to the *mi'r'aj*, meaning "ladder"—and was thought to have occurred in 621.

"One mighty in power," comes down from heaven to instruct the Prophet (Q 53:5). Sells combines vv. 5–7 and offers this elegant translation:

> This is a revelation taught him by one of great power and strength, that stretched out over while on the highest horizon.[2]

This figure steadily approaches him. He begins in the highest heaven, poised to come down (Q 53:6). Then he descends (Q 53:8). Then he approaches within two bow-lengths (Q 53:9). Presumably a bow-length is the distance an arrow can cover when shot from a bow. Finally he arrives at his destination. The narrator insists upon the authenticity of the account at the outset of his story.

> It is nothing but revelation revealed . . .[3] (Q 53:4)

Verse 4 begins the narrative. At the story's end, the narrator concludes,

> He revealed to his slave what he revealed. (Q 53:10; my trans.)[4]

I confess to some bewilderment, even irritation when I read these lines. The statements are too general to sustain the weight of the narrative.

---

1. For instance, Ezekiel's (Ezek 1), Saint Paul's (2 Cor 12), and John's (Rev 1).

2. Sells, *Approaching the Qur'an*, 44.

3. Droge: "an inspiration inspired."

4. The remaining two verses (vv. 17 and 18), while part of the story, consist of the narrator yet again claiming the authenticity of the preceding narrative.

They border on the tautological. What was it exactly that this powerful being taught to God's slave? What knowledge did God bring from the other world? This obscuring language exemplifies my first category of concealment. Rather than give information, the statements are an evasion, a taunt. This quote from René Girard (1923–2015) describes a situation analogous to these verses:

> It shows the disciple the gates of paradise and forbids him to enter with one and the same gesture.[5]

That is the reader's experience when she encounters both this first Qur'anic tale and the other stories I will examine. This is my theme in this chapter: Revelation in these passages denies the reader's access to that which is revealed.

The Second Story from Surat-al-Najm

In this story, the Prophet is lifted up to heaven, called here "the Garden of Refuge" (Q 53:15).[6] The "Lote Tree of Boundary" (v. 14) is thought to be either the boundary between earth and heaven or alternatively the boundary beyond which only God and not even the angels may pass.

Although the lote tree (also called buckthorn) is a common tree in the Middle East, shapely but ordinary, *this* tree is unique, similar to the tree of life in Genesis 2–3. This lote tree is analogous to the *axis mundi*, the world tree that runs through the center of the earth in many ancient mythologies. However, this tree is not at the center but rather at a boundary. An interpreter from the Sufi tradition observes:

> The mystery by the Mystery Itself, at the Lote Tree of the Boundary, that is the tree at which the knowledge of everyone comes to an end.[7]

The narrator tells the reader in the concluding verse:

> Certainly he saw one of the greatest signs of his Lord. (Q 53:18)

What did he see? What was the sign? One finds some sort of answer in the climactic verse:

---

5 From Girard, *Deceit, Desire, and the Novel,* quoted in Harrison, "The Prophet of Envy." In the original context, Girard was speaking of envy, which in the novels he discussed both motivated and disappointed the characters.

6. For reasons not clear to me, the author calls this "a descent" (Q 53:13).

7. Wains, "Trees," 361.

when (there) covered the Lote Tree what covered (it). (Q 53:16)

However, this verse raises so many questions: What covered the Lote Tree? Who placed the covering on the Lote Tree? What does the cover over the Lote Tree conceal? Can the Prophet see under the cover? What is the nature of the cover itself? The reader does not see, nor does she know exactly what the cover conceals. The Prophet's view does not turn aside. It does not transgress (Q 53:17). Compare to the opening line:

Your companion has not gone astray and has not erred. (Q 53:2)

These four negated verbs ("did not turn aside," "nor did it transgress," "has not gone astray," and "nor has he erred") say roughly the same thing. In what way did his *view* stay on the straight and narrow? Regarding the Prophet's gaze, either (a) he did not look at what was under the cover of the Lote Tree, (b) he did look at what was under the cover of the Lote Tree, (c) he looked at the covered Lote Tree and nothing else, or (d) he looked at the Lote Tree uncovered and nothing else. In (a) and (b) the emphasis is on whether or not the Prophet saw what was under the cover. Options (c) and (d) emphasize whether or not the Prophet looked at anything *other* than the Lote Tree in that forbidden place. The verbal ambiguity drains these three verses of any content. From the first story:

It is nothing but revelation revealed. (Q 53:4; my trans.)

And a similar verse comes a little later:

He revealed to his slave what he revealed. (Q 53:10; my trans.)

And from the second story:

It covered the Lote Tree what covered. (Q 53:16)

These verses disappoint because they promise much and reveal nothing. They function each in a similar manner. The three verses 4, 10, and 16 have these two things in common. First, they employ the same root twice in the same sentence: ("revelation" and "revealed" in v. 4; "then he revealed" and "he revealed" in v. 10; and "cover" and "what covers" in v. 16. In addition to these twice-used roots, they also each convey little information. These verses refuse to pull back the curtain. Or as Girard would say, they "show the gate of Paradise and forbid entrance with one and the same gesture."[8]

8. From Girard, *Deceit, Desire, and the Novel*, quoted in Harrison, "The Prophet of Envy."

Exodus 3

The burning bush narrative in Exodus has a similar phrase. It too repeats a keyword and reveals nothing. Moses asks God to disclose God's name. God answers:

> I am who I am. (Exod 3:14)

Note here, same as in the Sura, the double use of a keyword; here, "I am" ('*ehyeh*) is repeated, connected by a relative pronoun. In this passage too God refuses to divulge sacred information, in this case, God's true name. God responds to Moses's request by saying in effect, "None of your business." These verses in Exodus and Surat-al-Najm engage in a kind of theological double-talk—"revelation revealed," "it covered what covered," and "I am who I am." These enigmatic pronouncements each conceals a holy mystery, a divine teaching, a prophetic vision, or a sacred name of power. They cover up exactly what the reader wants to know.

After examining concealment by "obscuring language" in the first section, I now address the second category of concealment, a physical covering where God or heavenly beings place or create a physical barrier to conceal access to the divine presence. The protagonist is kept from seeing.

PHYSICAL COVERING

Exodus 33

Although not strictly a call narrative, Exodus 33 has many parallels to the burning bush story.[9] In Exodus 3 Moses asks:

> If I come to the Israelites and say to them, "The God of your ancestors has sent me to you," and they ask me, "What is his name?" what shall I say to them? (Exod 3:13)

In chapter 33, Moses asks,

> Show me your glory. (Exod 33:18)

The first question, "What is his name?" reflects the ancient belief that names, particularly names of gods, contain and embody the power in that person or deity. To know a name is in some way to be able to exercise control over the bearer of that name. For instance, the prophet Elisha cursed a group of children "in Yahweh's name," and as a result, two bears came out

9. An account in Q 7:143 tells a similar story to the narrative in Exod 33.

of the woods and slaughtered them (2 Kgs 2:23–25).[10] Asking to see God's glory is the same as asking God's name.

God warns Moses:

> . . . you cannot see my face; for no one shall see me and live.
> (Exod 33:20)

In these Exodus stories, Moses requests access to God's inner being. God refuses both times. In Exodus 33 God creates a physical barrier that separates Moses from the divine presence. God puts Moses in a shallow cave, and places a divine hand over the opening, covering it.

> . . . while my glory passes by I will put you in a cleft of the rock,
> and I will cover you with my hand until I have passed by.
> (Exod 33:22)

After passing, God removes the hand and permits Moses to see God's backside only.

> . . . then I will take away my hand, and you shall see my back; but
> my face shall not be seen. (Exod 33:23)

In Exodus 33, the narrator shuts the door of paradise against the reader by means of a physical barrier. This differs from using obscuring language (such as "I am who I am;" or "revelation revealed"). In Exodus 33, what stands between Moses and a revelation of God's glory is God's massive hand.

The Second Story from Surat-al-Najm

In the second Qur'anic story, something covers the Lote Tree. The contemporary reader does not know what it is:

> When (there) covers the Lote Tree what covers (it). (Q 53:16)

At the beginning of the narrative, the Lote Tree is merely a place marker. The Prophet receives his sign by the Garden of Refuge, (Q 53:15) "at the Lote Tree of Boundary" (Q 53:14). The "Garden" represents the larger area while the Lote Tree is an object in the garden. Both prepositions, "at" and "by," are spatial indicators signifying proximity. The word "garden" usually refers to the heavenly paradise. Although here it has the unusual qualifier "garden *of refuge*," there is no reason to think this is a different garden than

---

10. For a detailed discussion of this passage, see Penchansky, *What Rough Beast?*, chapter 6.

the others described in the Qur'an, the Garden of Eden and the Garden of Paradise.

The meaning of the Lote Tree shifts when the narrator says:

"It covers the Lote Tree what covers." (Q 53:16)

Now the Lote Tree has become the center of focus. The Lote Tree, part of the furniture of heaven, is covered. No one may see it because it is too holy to see. The Lote Tree stands for God. God is not depicted as a physical presence in Qur'anic writing. As a result, often when the Qur'an addresses edgy questions, an object or a person takes the place of God as a kind of stand-in.[11] Seeing the Lote Tree unveiled would be as dangerous as seeing inside the ark of the covenant in the Hebrew Bible,[12] or viewing God's face in Exodus 33. The cover on the Lote Tree conceals the divine presence.

Isaiah 6

In another call narrative, this one in the book of Isaiah, the prophet enters the temple. There he encounters an indeterminate number of angels, the seraphim. They have six wings each, but use only two for flight. The other two pairs are used to cover—two cover the angels' faces, and two cover their feet (which most scholars understand as a circumlocution for their genitals[13]).

It is unclear the purpose for the angels covering their faces and genitals. It is further unclear whether the seraphim conceal their faces from God or from Isaiah. If the angels are concealing their faces and genitals from God, it is because they acknowledge that even they are impure before God. More likely, the angels conceal their faces and genitals because they (who behold the face of God) are too holy for Isaiah to see, the face and genitals stand for the whole of their personal identity. The oddity of this detail is that although not permitted to view the private parts of angels, Isaiah is able to see God. The actions of the seraphim resemble the Qur'anic description of someone,

11. See also Chapter 5 (above), where the Stranger is called "servant of God," Chapter 6 (above), where Solomon fills this role, and here in Chapter 8, with the appearance of "one mighty in power."

12. "The descendants of Jeconiah did not rejoice with the people of Beth-shemesh when they greeted the ark of the LORD; and he killed seventy men of them. The people mourned because the LORD had made a great slaughter among the people" (1 Sam 6:19), although the translation is not certain. The film *Raiders of the Lost Ark*, consistent with the biblical text, portrays those who view the ark's insides dying a horrible death.

13. For other examples of feet standing in for genitals, see Exod 4:25; Deut 26:57; Ruth 3:3–14; 1 Sam 24:3; 2 Sam 11:8.

probably God, who hides the Lote Tree from Muhammad. In both cases, the angels' wings and the covering over the Lote Tree, conceal raw unmediated holiness from eyes either not capable of seeing or not worthy to see. The covering separates what is holy from that which is insufficiently holy.

Isaiah 6 is written in the first person, and the author makes a dramatic claim. Although not permitted to see angel faces and angel "feet," he declares:

> I saw the Lord ['adonay]. (Isa 6:1)

And later, employing the sacred name of the God of Israel, he says:

> . . . my eyes have seen the King, the LORD [Yahweh] of hosts! (Isa 6:5)

The emphasis is on sight. The rest of the passage describes what he sees. Surat-al-Najm also emphasizes the "gaze" of the Prophet, using words referring to sight four times:

> His heart did not lie about what it saw. Will you dispute with him about what he sees? (Q 53:11–12) His sight did not turn aside, nor did it transgress. (Q 53:17) Certainly he saw one of the greatest signs of his Lord. (Q 53:18)

There is no covering that separates Isaiah from the beatific vision. However, Isaiah conceals from the reader his view of the holy God. Perhaps, Isaiah is reticent because when he sees God, he is horrified at the danger it puts him in. He says:

> Woe is me! I am lost, for I am a man of unclean lips, and I live among a people of unclean lips; yet my eyes have seen the King, the LORD of hosts!

Isaiah fears because he has seen something forbidden. As God said to Moses,

> . . . no one shall see me and live. (Exod 33:20)

Isaiah devotes many words to describing the angels, and to describing the effects of Yahweh's presence in the temple. However, Isaiah finds no speech for God's appearance. There are two acts of concealment in the passage. First, the angels conceal their person from Isaiah. Second, Isaiah conceals his vision of Yahweh from the reader. In a sense, the entire passage deals in concealment. Smoke fills the temple (Isa 6:4), which obscures the sight and hides powerful and mysterious things.[14] The angels employ two-thirds of their wings to cover parts of their bodies—face and groin (Isa 6:2). Finally, although the prophet proclaims, "I saw Yahweh," there is no physical description of deity, although clearly God is a physical presence, whose garment "fills" an earthly space. The closest to a description of God is the angelic proclamation of God's attributes and titles,

> Holy, holy, holy is the LORD of hosts;
>   the whole earth is full of his glory. (Isa 6:3)

However, one reads no actual description of what the prophet sees (other than the peripherals of smoke and the edge of the divine garment).[15] The angelic presences, the seraphim, all have the same complement of wings and the same role in the liturgical choir. God maintains his otherness in this tale of divine appearance, because the narrator, the prophet himself, never describes deity. The reader does not know, cannot know, what exactly he has seen.

AMBIGUITY OF CHARACTER

The third category of covering, narrative ambiguity, is when the identity of a key figure in the narrative is somehow confused or problematized, kept from either the prophet or the reader or both.

The First Story from Surat-al-Najm

In the beginning narrative of Surat-al-Najm, the climax occurs when the divine figure has moved from heaven to earth, approaching ever closer, until he in fact reaches the Prophet. Who is this divine figure? It is not identified in the text. The drama builds up slowly after the introductory summary statement:

> It is nothing but revelation revealed. (Q 53:4; my trans.)

---

14. This probably refers to the same phenomenon as the "hem of his robe," which fills the temple in Isa 6:1. Both smoke (Isa 6:4) and robe (Isa 6:1) are said in different places to fill the temple.

15. The conversation between the prophet and Yahweh that follows (Isa 6:6–13), although connected to the temple vision, constitutes a significant change in tone and topic. I will not examine it here.

The figure is described in his potency, about to descend (Q 53:6). Then he appears on the horizon (Q 53:7). Then he draws near and comes down (Q 53:8). Then he comes even closer (Q 53:9; my trans.), and then, and then . . . he

. . . reveals what he reveals. (Q 53:10; my trans.)

The narrator describes the figure as

. . . one harsh in power. (Q 53:5)

From the beginning, Islamic scholars have argued: Is it God who has come down and taught the Prophet, or the angel Gabriel? Those who argue that it is God note that the phrase "mighty in power" more likely refers to God than to an angel. See for instance:

Yet they dispute about God, yet he is mighty in power." (Q 13:13)

A second reason to identify the figure as God is that this verse describes Muhammad as "his slave":

He revealed to his slave what he revealed. (Q 53:10; my trans.)

Muhammad was never a slave of Gabriel, but rather in the Qur'an he frequently is called a slave of God. For instance, the Prophet identifies himself:

I am a servant [slave] of God. (Q 19:30)

Despite this, the majority of Islamic interpreters identify the figure as Gabriel. This is because the description is too physical, too material to portray the infinite God who in Islam has no physical body. This divine visitor hangs in the sky and then comes down, being two bow-lengths distant (Q 53:9), which describes a being with a physical body who appears in one place and moves to a different space.

The wider Islamic tradition regards the angel Gabriel as the one who brings revelation to the Prophet, and so Islamic interpreters tend to read Gabriel back into Surat-al-Najm as well—this despite the theological problems it raises. The figure is not named. At the level of the text itself as opposed to the later accretion of tradition, the ambiguity remains as to the identity of "one mighty in power." The words of the text positively resist any certitude.

Exodus 3

The burning bush narrative in Exodus 3 also problematizes the identity of the divine figure but in a different manner. In v. 2, the narrator identifies the voice from the burning bush as "the angel of Yahweh." Moments later the narrator states,

> *God* called to him out of the bush . . . (Exod 3:4, italics added)

And later the voice from the bush says,

> I am the *God* of your fathers. . . (Exod 3:6, italics added)

In sum, Exodus 3 obscures the identity of the divine voice by referring to it in two conflicting ways, as "the angel of Yahweh" and as "the God of your fathers." In the sura, the designation "one mighty in power" functions in a similar manner. Both texts obscure the identity of the divine power so as to mystify God's appearance. Thus, God is less physical, more abstract because mediated and not direct. To think otherwise risks diminishing God. In the case of Islam, one becomes guilty of the sin of comparison, *shirk,* if one describes God in human terms, as having a body. Most Muslim interpreters identify Gabriel as the messenger. Even so, this identity-obscuring strategy resists the reader easily settling on God or Gabriel. This verbal ambiguity too is a kind of covering. Such concealment functions to elevate the mysterious nature of the divine appearance. It avoids the kind of idolatry in surrounding cultures. This kind of concealment eschews making an image and emphasizes the division between the divine and the human realm.[16]

These ancient writers provide a mechanism that explains how a transcendent and powerful God condescends to human companionship. By transcendent I mean beyond and outside of the human realm. These Qur'anic and biblical texts articulate different strategies by which they resolve the problem of divine encounter. As a theological problem, these texts ask, How can a transcendent God communicate to a finite human? Does God have a shape? Does God occupy specific space in the material world? As a linguistic problem, they ask, What language should one use to describe God in a divine encounter? Likewise, as a narrative problem they ask, How does one tell a story that has God as a character?

16. There is of course a simpler explanation for the disparity between "the angel of Yahweh" and "the God of your fathers" in Exodus 3. One might see this confusion as the result of the text passing through two different editorial processes—one editor more comfortable with the actual God appearing, rather than a representative. A second editor required that an angel serve as buffer between God and Moses. Even so, the text exists and continues to be read in its present complex, contradictory form. The final editor, whoever that might have been, apparently was comfortable with the created ambiguity.

Surat-al-Najm and Exodus 3 are reticent to nail down the identity of the divine visitor. Isaiah in contrast, claims to have actually seen Yahweh. However, he does not describe what he sees. Exodus 33 shows God physically present but concealed from Moses *and* the reader by God's enormous hand. I shall not propose, as many do, a chronological explanation or a model of evolutionary development to explain these different modes of understanding. Many see in texts such as these evidence of a transition over time from a strongly anthropomorphic deity at the beginning to an abstract deity with angelic intermediaries as a buffer at a later "more sophisticated" stage. Rather, these texts represent different strategies by which one might describe the divine character. Obscuring language, physical covering, and ambiguity of character each offers a scenario for how one might describe the divine encounter. These strategies probably existed at the same time, or else they appeared in no particular order. They each in their own way deconstruct the very idea of revelation. The *absence* of key information is the key feature of these passages. I will repeat that. The *absence* of key information is the leading feature of these passages. Their hollowed-out climaxes suggest that revelation is not so much the unveiling of truth. Rather, the authors snatch the mysteries away from the reader at the moment of revelation.

There is one more passage to consider. In Exodus 34, Moses comes down from the mountain after speaking to God. When he addresses the people,

[T]he skin of his face was shining. (Exod 34:30)

It frightens his audience. Therefore, he covers his face with a veil. When he speaks to God he removes the veil. That veil is like the covering of the Lote Tree, like God's massive hand keeping Moses from seeing divine glory, like the seraphim wings that obscure Isaiah's sight. Revelation in these passages is about covering as much as revealing. With rare exceptions in these texts, divine holiness is not for human eyes.

Surat- ʿAbasa Q 80

In the name of God, the Merciful, the Compassionate. He frowned and turned away because the blind man came to him. What will make you know? Perhaps he will yet purify himself, or take heed and the Reminder will benefit him. [He might remember your teaching and reap benefit from it.—dp] As for the one who considers himself independent, you give your attention to him, Yet it is not dependent on you if he does not purify himself. But as for the one who comes running to you, and who fears God, from him you are distracted.

9

Surat-'Abasa (He Frowned)

Q 80—The Prophet and the Blind Man

Texts in comparison: Luke 18:35–38; Mark 10:46–52;
Matthew 20:29–34

MUHAMMAD AND THE BLIND MAN

Surat- 'Abasa drops the reader in the middle of a narrative. It begins,

He frowned and turned away. (Q 80:1).

The sura is named from the first word in this verse, *'abasa*, "he frowned."
Two questions immediately arise—First, *who* is the figure who frowned and
turned away? Second, *why* did he frown and turn away? The Qur'an does not
answer the first question. Although it is *conceivable* that the verse describes
an anonymous or hypothetical person, the earliest traditions identify this
figure without question as the Prophet Muhammad. Although I am skepti-
cal of how later Islamic tradition fills in the gaps in Qur'anic stories, in this
case the identification is likely correct. The connection of the story to the
Prophet Muhammad and his leadership is early and persuasive. Therefore,
I will assume that this main character in the sura, the one who frowned, is
the Prophet Muhammad, and I will refer to him as such. The ancient reader

156

would not have questioned this identification. Now I proceed to the second question: Why did he frown and turn away?

In addition to the Prophet, there are three other characters in the narrative: a blind man, a rich man, and one other. The final character is the divine voice that challenges the Prophet and enlarges his perspective. When we consider the second question—Why did the Prophet turn away?—v. 2 gives the answer. Although coming after it in the order of verses, what happens in v. 2, chronologically, would have occurred first, coming before the Prophet's frown, in v. 1. He frowned and turned away, we are told,

> . . . when the blind man came. (Q 80:2; my trans.)

The frown, an involuntary action, indicates the Prophet's inward displeasure when he turned. The turning away is a willful act, a deliberate rejection of the blind man's importunity.

Muhammad expresses his displeasure at being interrupted. Although he turns away from the blind man, he pursues another, described as a "self-sufficient one."[1] I translate the Arabic word as "rich man" because he appears to have no needs material or spiritual. He asks nothing from the Prophet, or from anyone else. The Prophet pays attention to this rich man. The blind man, needy and eager, stands in stark contrast. Muhammad's behavior toward the blind man follows a pattern:

> Whenever he [the blind man] comes around, you [Muhammad]
> act distracted [literally, "you are distracted *from* him"]. (Q 80:10;
> my trans./para.)

However, Muhammad treats the rich man differently.

> For you pay attention to him. (Q 80:6; my trans.).[2]

There is a strong difference between the two verbs that describe Muhammad's disposition toward those two. He "gives attention to" the rich man and "is distracted from," the blind man. Note too the use of the prepositions "to" or "toward" the rich man, and "off, away from" the blind man. The two prepositions take the subject in opposite directions, underscoring the distancing between them. These movements are best understood spatially. The blind man moves *toward* the Prophet. The Prophet moves *away from* the blind man, or at least turns in the opposite direction. The rich man might be said to walk alongside the Prophet, but actually the rich man does not move

1. Later tradition identifies him as an important member of the Quraysh, the ruling tribe. Muhammad too belonged to this tribe.

2. Droge: "you give your attention to him." I preferred the more colloquial "pay attention."

at all—not toward the Prophet, as does the blind man, not turning away. Finally, the Prophet moves toward the rich man. These reactions are the exact opposite of how the Prophet should act, according to the divine voice.

God makes four statements addressed to the Prophet. The first concerns the blind man. Regarding the blind man God asks:

> How can you know whether he [the blind man] might purify himself? (Q 80:3; my trans.)

God further suggests that the blind man might have benefited from the Prophet's teaching (Q 80:4). This is my paraphrase of Q 80:4. Concerning the blind man, God says:

> Or he might remember, so that the memory benefits him [that is, the memory of what Muhammad might have said to the blind man].[3]

In the second statement concerning the blind man, God observes:

> But as for the one [that is, the blind man] who comes to you running. (Q 80:8; my trans.)

Concerning the rich man the voice says:

> But as for the rich man, you pay attention to him. (Q 80:5; my trans.) [and]
> It is no concern of yours if he does not purify himself. (Q 80:7; my trans.)

By these four sentences, God speaks against Muhammad's decision to prefer the rich man to the blind man. Muhammad's concern to "purify" the rich man is ill-placed, and he has failed to consider this transformation of the blind man.

Muhammad assumes that there would be no benefit by attending to the blind man. On what basis does he draw that conclusion? The case of the rich man is different. The Prophet believes he has a responsibility to oversee the purification of the rich man. He might even believe at that moment that he has the power in himself to accomplish the man's purification. It is important for Muhammad, and his community strongly desired that this prominent man be purified.

I must here address the meaning of "purify." The word is used about both the blind man and the rich man. "Purify" in English might imply a ritual such as washing, although that meaning does not apply here. A cognate

---

3. Droge's translation of this difficult verse is awkward: "and the Reminder will benefit him," referring to the Qur'an as a reminder (421n5).

word in the Hebrew Bible speaks of a cleansing from sin. The Hebrew root *z-k-h* means to be clear, pure, justified; to be bright, clean. In the book of Job the word is used:

> What are mortals, that they can be *clean*?
>> Or those born of women, that they can be righteous?
>> (Job 15:14, italics added)
> How can one born of women be *pure*? (Job 25:4, italics added)

And in the book of Psalms:

> . . . purge me and I shall be *clean*.
> (Ps 51:6; italics added)

> In vain I have kept my heart *clean*.
> (Ps 73:13; italics added)

> How can young people keep their way *pure*?
> (Ps 119:9, italics added)

And in Proverbs:

> Who can say I have made my heart *clean*?
> (Prov 20:9, italics added)

Most translate the Arabic word as "purify," but in English that implies a cultic activity comparable to the Christian rite of baptism or the Islamic washing ritual, *wudu*. In this verse, it seems to be a more general term for one who has had her sins forgiven and is now included in the community of faith. Thus, in this sura "purify" seems a more general term to describe a believer.

God tells the Prophet that he knows nothing about the blind man's potential. God speaks differently about the Prophet's attitude toward the rich man. God informs the Prophet that the Prophet himself is not responsible for the rich man's purification. Muhammad lacks the power. The way that the Prophet regards the rich man usurps what should be under God's purview alone. These sentences indicate that God favors the blind man. Although it is more common in Islam to declare that people stand before God as equal, in this sura the rich man stands lower in God's estimation than the blind man. The blind man is *more* likely to become purified than the rich man, and thus God prefers him.[4]

The contrast in Muhammad's attitude toward the two men is intensified by the first words in each of these parallel verses:

---

4. Roman Catholics' "preferential option for the poor" originates from a similar impulse.

But as for the rich man . . . (Q 80:5; my trans.)

But as for the one [that is, the blind man] who comes to you
running . . . (Q 80:8; my trans.)

They share the introductory phrase ("what about the one who . . ." or
"regarding the one who"). They lay out the two objects of the Prophet's attention. God draws the Prophet's attention to the disparity between his treatment
of the rich man when compared to his snub of the blind man. When God asks:

What about the rich man? (Q 80:5)

he does not mean that the Prophet has forgotten or not noticed him. Rather,
Muhammad has ignored the disparity between his treatment of the two individuals. When God says:

But as for the one who comes to you running . . .
(Q 80:8; my trans.)

it is not that the Prophet overlooked the blind man. Rather, the divine voice
wants to draw the Prophet's attention to a different interpretation of the
blind man's running. For the Prophet, when the blind man runs up to him, it
is an interruption, an annoyance, an irritation. In contrast, the divine voice
regards the running as a window into the blind man's intention and sincer-
ity. God gives one final description of the blind man, that

. . . he fears [God]. (Q 80:9; my trans.)[5]

The rich man contrasts sharply with the blind man. He is self-sufficient, while the blind man, whose need is so great, not only comes; he *runs*
to the Prophet. By running, he therefore gives every indication of receptivity
to the Prophet's message. To review:

He *comes* to the Prophet (Q 80:2)

he *runs* to the Prophet (Q 80:8)

he *fears* God (Q 80:9)

The choice between the two men should have been obvious. The
Prophet decided incorrectly, and God rebukes him.

Rather than commanding the Prophet to befriend the blind man, God
only observes with disapproval his actions in how he shows preference for
the rich man. Giving special attention to the rich man is pointless, because

5. The word "God" is not in the Arabic text but is implied by the common use of
the verb, "he fears."

that man does not think he needs anything. Muhammad misses an opportunity for a true convert by wasting his time on a hopeless case. More than that, Muhammad has chosen the lesser individual. In his neediness, the blind man is a better person, but the Prophet wants the rich man to convert to Islam. The man's importance in the social hierarchy would greatly benefit the beleaguered Islamic community. Islamic tradition explains that Muhammad greatly desired to gain the support of Meccan leadership. All the time, however, there is one right next to him, pursuing him, wanting to learn, eager to submit.

God admonishes the Prophet not to waste his time on a self-sufficient person who does not need or does not believe that he needs the revelation. The Synoptic Gospels in the New Testament suggest a similar sentiment. Jesus tells the Pharisees:

> It is not the well who need a physician. (Mark 2:17)[6]

Likewise, in the Gospel of John, Jesus says:

> If you were blind, you would have no sin. But now that you say "We see," your sin remains. (John 9:41)

In the Qur'an, the self-sufficient one lacks the humility to submit to God.

JESUS AND THE BLIND MAN

A narrative found in all three Synoptic Gospels[7] strongly resembles this Qur'anic story. As Jesus passes through a crowd, a blind man[8] shouts:

> Son of David, have mercy on me. (Luke 18:18)

The crowd shushes him. In the Gospel of Mark, it says:

> Many sternly ordered him to be quiet. (Mark 10:48)

COMPARISON OF THE TWO STORIES

The same word is used in all three Gospels for what the crowd says: *epetimōn/epetimēsen.* It means to "strongly admonish." When Jesus hears, he intervenes, calls the blind man to him, and heals him.

6. Also featured in Luke 5:31 and Matt 9:12

7. Luke 18:35–38; Mark 10:46–52; Matt 20:29–34

8. In Luke and Mark there is one blind man, while in Matthew there are two. However, in most other respects the synoptic versions are quite similar.

The similarities between the Qur'anic and the Gospel story are striking. I note six similarities.

1. Both stories feature blind men.

2. In both stories, the blind man pushes forward. In the sura he is described as running. In the Gospels he shouts.

3. In both stories the blind man shows more insight than those around
   him. In the sura, he "fears God." In the Gospels he addresses Jesus
   using a messianic title, "Son of David."

4. In each story, the blind man is admonished for an inappropriate and
   disrespectful approach to the prophet. In the sura, the Prophet "frowns."
   In the Gospels the blind man is "sternly warned." He is of lower status,
   and so attention paid to him is a waste of time.

5. In both stories a divine authority intervenes to elevate the status of the
   blind man. Thus he is deemed worthy of the prophet's attention. In the
   Gospels, Jesus intervenes; in the Qur'an, the divine voice steps in.

6. In both stories—in the Gospels as well as the Qur'anic account—the
   reader sympathizes with the blind man. Persons whom the larger society regards as having lower status both texts regard as most important.

In my initial research I was reluctant to bring together these passages
from the Qur'an and the Bible. I have no desire to measure Jesus against
Muhammad. However, I found an approach that would help me navigate
the interreligious minefield I had set out for myself. It requires one assumption that I believe is well-founded: the Qur'an's original audience would
have been familiar with this Gospel story in some form.

That raises an important question—why would the early Islamic community preserve and venerate a story in the Qur'an that reflects poorly on
the Prophet? This question becomes more intense when one assumes that
the first readers of the sura were aware that in the Christian story Jesus
neither frowns nor turns away from the blind man. The assumption behind
this question is wrong, however, for it misunderstands the Qur'an's intention. Muhammad in the Qur'anic narrative does not function in the same
way that Jesus does in the Gospels. Rather, Muhammad's role, frowning
and turning away from the blind man, resembles the role of the crowd in
the Gospel story—the ones who strongly admonish the blind man to be
quiet. The role of Jesus in the Gospels is filled in the Qur'anic narrative by
the divine voice. As Jesus admonishes the crowds who sought to silence
the blind man, so the divine voice admonishes the Prophet. Thus the sura
and the Gospels share the same basic ethical position—that the faithful

community should attend to its weaker members, those of lower status. In the case of the Gospels, that value is expressed by the statement and actions of Jesus, who says to the crowd,

> . . . call him here, (Mark 10:49)

and to the blind man,

> what do you want me to do for you? (Mark 10:51)

In the case of the sura, it is the voice who corrects the Prophet and challenges him to express care for the outsider.

This understanding of the Qur'anic narrative (that the divine voice corrects the Prophet) would have well served the early Islamic community. It affirms a fundamental distinction Muslims make between themselves and the Christians: From an Islamic perspective, the Christians deified their leader and confused him with the divine.

The comparison highlights the contrast between the Prophet Muhammad, who fails to attend to a needy individual, and Jesus, who in the same situation meets the need. This reflects the early Islamic emphasis that Muhammad is a human and not a divine being.

Also relevant is this passage from the book of Acts:

> When the crowds saw what Paul had done they shouted. . ."the gods have come down to us. . ." When the apostles Barnabas and Saul heard of it, they tore their clothes and rushed into the crowd shouting, ". . . we are mortals like you." (Acts 14:11, 14, 15)

The sura insists that the Prophet too is a "mortal like you."

Jesus in the Gospel accounts attends to the blind man. However, the Gospels do not always portray Jesus reaching out to the marginalized. For instance, Jesus refuses to help the daughter of the Syrophoenician woman in Mark 7, saying,

> It is not fitting to give the children's bread to dogs. (Mark 7:27)

He only relents when the woman challenges him with self-effacing humor. The story of Jesus and the blind man juxtaposed with Surat-'Abasa, creates a picture of how the early Islamic community might have understood and transformed the earlier story from the Synoptic Gospels to serve their needs.

This is not the only instance when God corrects the Prophet. For example, Surat-al-Hajj allows for the possibility of prophetic error and provides the solution:[9]

> We have not sent any messenger or any prophet before you, except that, when he began to wish, Satan cast (something) into his wishful thinking.[10] But God cancels what Satan casts, (and) then God clearly composes His verses . . . (Q 22:52)

Consider also this passage:

> Surely they almost tempted you away from what We inspired you (with), so that you might forge against Us (something) other than it, and then they would indeed have taken you as a friend, And had We not made you (stand) firm, you would almost have been disposed toward them a little. (Q 17:73–74)

The brief narrative in Surat-ʿAbasa shows the Prophet human, and that on occasion he makes political decisions that divert from the basic principles of his professed faith. At those times God corrects him, and he humbly receives the correction. When the Islamic story first took form, the writer drew from a deep tradition of flawed prophets one finds in the Hebrew Bible. Moses murders an Egyptian (Exod 2:12). Noah gets drunk and exposes himself to his sons (Gen 9:20–24). Abraham pimps his wife to Pharaoh (Gen 12:10–15), and his son Isaac pimps *his* wife to the king of Gerar (Gen 26:1–11). David has sex with Bathsheba and then he murders her husband (2 Sam 11:2–27). In the New Testament, Peter betrays Christ to save his own life.

Subsequently, there developed in Islam the notion of ʿiṣma, the belief in the infallibility of the Prophet. It became necessary to distinguish between prophetic mistakes that were conceivable, and hypothetical prophetic sins that were considered impossible. The prophets might make mistakes, but it was inconceivable that a prophet would sin. Therefore, to preserve the distinction between *mistake* and *sin*, they drastically limited the definition of sin. A sin was thus defined as intentionally doing wrong with full knowledge.

However, there is not the slightest hint in the Qurʾanic narrative that justifies what the Prophet did. One finds no effort to exonerate, and there is no attempt in the narrative to categorize the Prophet's choices as not sin

---

9. I referred to this verse in Chapter 2.

10. This wishful thinking might tie in with the Prophet's desire to heal the breech between the Muslims and his tribe, the Quraysh.

but rather a mistake. The story ends with a final description of the Prophet's rejection of the blind man.

> When around the blind man you are distracted. (Q 80:10; my trans.)

If anything, the later Islamic tradition underscores the Prophet's culpability, recounting how the blind man, whom later tradition names Ibn Umm Maktum, rose to prominence within the Islamic community and died a martyr in battle though blind. According to this tradition, every time the Prophet encountered Ibn Umm Maktum, he would say, "Welcome to him on whose account my Lord rebuked me."[11] It was not thought disrespectful to acknowledge the Prophet's human fallibility and how the Prophet humbly accepted rebuke. He even joked about it.

There is in the sura an extraordinary honesty regarding the failings of the Prophet and the reasons and motivations for that failure—a desire for status, protection, and advancement for his new community. The Quraysh, the ruling tribe in Mecca, denigrated the early Islamic community as nothing but slaves and misfits. Because of this, the Prophet desired his powerful fellow Qurayshi to become Muslims. The incident in Surat-'Abasa represents an instance of this.[12]

This little story begins and ends in ambiguity. First, it begins in the middle of the action:

> He frowned and turned away. (Q 80:1)

Its ending leaves the reader hanging:

> Whenever the blind man comes around, you are distracted.
> (Q 80:10; my trans.)[13]

In the Qur'an, the reader never finds out how Muhammad reacts to this divine rebuke, or whether the blind man ever gains his attention.

The Prophet concerns himself with a rich and powerful person and ignores a poor, disabled beggar. It goes to the heart of Islamic ethics that one must at the very least treat all humans as equals before God. This is why God corrects the Prophet.

11. Quoted in Sale, trans., *The Koran*, 570.

12. See Chapter 2 for another example.

13. Droge: ". . . from him you are distracted."

Epilogue

The Qur'an is neither derivative nor uncreative. It stands with the other major world scriptures in its stature, insight, and beauty. In my ignorance, I had expected the Qur'an to be rigid and authoritarian. I found myself surprised by its humane understanding and challenging ethic. The scope of my study is limited in that I examined only the narrative genre, and a scant nine suras. From this admittedly limited sample of the Qur'an's writing, I offer the following reflections. These stories are characterized by ambiguity and nuance. Such qualities as these are essential for the continued relevance of the Qur'an over time. I noticed a tension between *tawḥid* (monotheism) and the Qur'an's depiction of the crowded realm of the spirit world. The Qur'an never denies God's goodness, but questions about God's goodness are legitimately raised in its pages. Perhaps most significantly, in these stories, God's message to humans is subject to the limitations of human language and human frailty. In its fabric the human and the divine are linked inextricably.

The Qur'an is a human document. This is not to question its divine origin or its divine qualities, but these ancient words are clearly rooted in their time and in the concerns of their human authors. As just one example, Surat-al-Masad was directed toward a single named individual, apparently a contemporary of the Prophet (Abu Lahab, see Chapter 4). The Qur'an is thoroughly human in all its aspects. Just as they do in the Jewish and Christian scriptures, so in the Qur'an the divine qualities of the text shine through this humanity rather than through humanity's absence. In this I respectfully diverge from orthodox Islam, where many claim that the entire Qur'an existed with God before any created thing, similar to how Proverbs 8 describes Ḥokmah. (See Chapter 2.)

I learned that in the Qur'an's portrayal of the Prophet Muhammad, he has much in common with prophets in the Bible. The Qur'an's Muhammad

166

has less congruence with subsequent Islamic understandings of the Prophet's life and teaching, which portray him as flawless.

While the Jewish, Christian, and Islamic religions change and adapt, their scriptures do not change. As a result, there emerges a disparity between the two, the scripture and those in a different time and place who follow the religion. This disparity creates problems for those later believers. When later beliefs conflict with things that their scripture says, that causes conflict. In some cases, what is fragmented and inchoate in the scripture becomes defined and systematized in later eras. For instance, in the Hebrew Bible the path to monotheism was slow and episodic. There are many passages that imply or assume the existence of other gods. Even the first commandment, often regarded as the monotheistic manifesto, says:

You shall have no other gods before me. (Exod 20:3)

This implies that other gods exist. However, they must not be worshiped alongside Yahweh, the God of Israel. That is a problem for monotheism. In the New Testament, one does not find full-blown expositions of the Holy Trinity or the dual nature of Christ. That creates a problem for Christianity. In a similar way the Qur'an openly questions itself regarding what later Islam says about monotheism (there is only one God), theodicy (all that God does is good; all that God says is true), and prophecy or revelation (the Prophet's message is a "clear book" [Q 27:1], an unmediated message from God).

Pious interpreters embed problematic stories such as the ones I covered here, in larger master narratives of their own creation. They depend on biographies and teachings of the Prophet written later than the Qur'an itself. These master narratives reflect subsequent concerns. By means of these overarching narratives, the interpreters redirect the meaning of the stories in less transgressive directions; alternatively, traditional interpretations marginalize or abrogate offending passages by interpreting them through the lens of less threatening verses. For instance, the innocent jinn listening to the heavenly council in seats reserved for them become "rebellious satans" eavesdropping where they never belonged. (See Chapter 3.) The pious interpreter regards these more conforming passages, those that disparage the jinn, as more authoritative. In another strategy, the interpreters avoid the troublesome texts altogether or only comment on a few pious statements within them while ignoring the import of the wholes.

The Qur'an is best approached by highlighting its ambiguity and the tension it creates. Using a metaphor of sound, we may say that the narratives I chose create dissonance in the mind of the reader. Dissonance is when two sounds clash, irritating to the ear. Elements of the narrative that do not

quite cohere together create dissonance in the experience of reading. For example, the three layers in the story of "the Companions of the Cave" do not
fit together smoothly. Some of the stories lack beginnings or endings. (See
Chapter 7.) Sometimes, elements of a narrative conflict with similar accounts
in other parts of the Qur'an or conflict with later interpretive traditions. At
times a narrative conflicts with a reader's expectation or moral stance. One
can harmonize dissonance of sound by supplying a resolving note or chord.
When reading the Qur'an, however, I allow the irritant to remain. This shows
respect for the actual words of the sura. Understanding the dissonance in
these narratives brings the interpreter to the place where meaning is formed.
The dissonance itself provides a key to how such meaning is produced and
how it affects the reader. Additionally, observing the dissonance allows the
interpreter to see traces of an unfiltered (or a less filtered) picture of Islam's
first generation.

This journey of discovery has always been a personal one for me. A
long time before I began this project, I was introduced to the story of Joseph
in the Qur'an (Q 12). This was my first real encounter with Islam's book.
Like the Bible's Joseph story, the Joseph Sura is a long, continuous narrative,
and it roughly parallels the biblical account.[1] There is, however, one incident
in the Qur'an's account not found in Genesis, and this incident gave me a
first inkling that the Qur'an had qualities I wanted to investigate. It concerns
the wife of the high Egyptian official. Her husband is named Potiphar in the
Bible, but she remains unnamed in the Qur'an. The woman has become an
subject of gossip among the other noblewomen because of her obsession
with Joseph. To regain her reputation, she invites them all to a party at her
house and provides them food and utensils. At the banquet, she parades
Joseph before them. He is so gorgeous that all the women, overwhelmed
with passion for the young man, cut themselves accidentally. They tell their
hostess that now they can understand and sympathize with her infatuation
with her slave.

It is a funny story. Also, it offers multilayered characterization and
deep irony, with a narrative voice that winks at the reader, in on the joke.
I wondered if perhaps I was wrong. The Qur'an was not the dour writing I
had expected.

In the Introduction I wrote of what drew me to the Qur'an. Muslims
claim that any open-minded examination of the Qur'an will render its
uniqueness apparent and give incontrovertible proof of its divine origin.
However, if one reads the Qur'an in translation, beginning with the first
sura, the result will be disappointing. One can easily get lost in the details

1. John Kaltner's *Inquiring of Joseph* is an excellent and detailed analysis of this tale.

and the strangeness of first encounter. After reading the first sura, a brief prayer, the second sura, Al-Bakara, overwhelms. It is the longest sura of the Qur'an, and it jumps to many different subjects. The eyes of the average reader will likely glaze over and miss the essentials.

Reading the Qur'an in English translation does not seem adequate as a means to access the Qur'an's sublimity. The difference between the Qur'an in translation and the Qur'an in its original Arabic is so profound that Muslims usually do not call an English version a *translation* but rather an *interpretation*. The importance of the Qur'an in Arabic to Muslims is much greater than the comparative importance for Jews and Christians of the original languages of their scriptures. So, I learned Arabic. I do not know it well enough to speak, unfortunately, but I can read the Qur'an with a good dictionary. Muslims are indeed correct—The Qur'an in Arabic is nuanced and beautiful. One notices details, features that do not easily translate. As just one example, the last line in a given sura almost always ends in a rhyme. This and much else is lost in English renderings.

However, reading the Qur'an in Arabic was not sufficient. I had to somehow approach the experience of the Qur'an like a Muslim. Reaching for that experience, I memorized Surat-al-Najm and Surat-'Abasa when I began my research on those suras. Having memorized them, I then learned to chant the suras using a program I found on the internet. At first my chanting was halting and difficult, but after a while it became effortless, almost unconscious. I experienced these sacred words flowing freely out of my mouth in the ancient rhythm and cantillation. Then I got *it*. Or at least I got the beginning of *it* because I experienced the special power of the Qur'an. The impact of people over the centuries chanting the same verses in communities throughout the world adds weight to the words. When I chanted those verses, I found that I was not alone. I joined a mighty river made up of all the people who chanted the same sura before me and were chanting it even as I did. I was only able to go ankle-deep in that river, but I felt the tug of its current. Chanting the Qur'an greatly enriched my understanding of these suras. I began to notice every turn of phrase, every ambiguity and misdirection. It was meditative. It was prayer.

The Qur'an and the Bible are quite dissimilar. Even though I compare them and find many points of commonality, I am still struck by how different they are from each other in tone, style, and intention. Notwithstanding, they both draw from the same mythic pool, or we might say they drink from the same well. It makes little difference to the Muslim community that I am impressed with their Qur'an. But it means a great deal to me.

And now that I have come to the end of my book, I realize that I have scarcely begun.

Bibliography[1]

Abu Zayd, Nasr Hamid. "Everyday Life." In *EQ* 2:80–97.

Ahmed, Shahab. "Satanic Verses." In *EQ* 4:531–36.

Ali, Abdullah Yusuf, trans. *The Holy Qur'an: Text, Translation*. Elmhurst: Tahrike Tarsile Qur'an, 2001.

Ali, Mir Ahmed, trans. *The Holy Qur'an: The Final Testament; Arabic Text with English Translation and Commentary*. Elmhurst, NY: Tahrike Tarsile Qur'an, 2009.

Al-Kalbi, Ibn Hisham. *The Book of Idols*. Translated by Nabih Amin Faris. Princeton: Princeton University Press, 1952.

An-Nabbi, Tibb. *Medicine of the Prophet*. London: Ta-Ha, 1994.

Asad, Muhammad. *The Message of the Qur'an*. Gibraltar: Dar al-Andalus, 1980.

Austin, R. W. J. "Al-Gharaniq Al-'Ula—The Twilight of the Arabian Goddess." *A Miscellany of Middle Eastern Articles: In Memoriam Thomas Muir Johnstone 1924–1983*, edited by A. K. Irvine et al., 15–21. London: Longman, 1988.

Ayoub, Mahmoud M. *The Qur'an and Its Interpreters*. Albany: State University of New York Press, 1984.

Bell, Richard. *A Commentary on the Qur'an*. 2 vols. Journal of Semitic Studies Monographs 14. Manchester: University of Manchester, 1991.

Boda, Mark J., Michael H. Floyd, and Colin M. Toffelmire, eds. *The Book of the Twelve and the New Form Criticism*. Ancient Near East Monographs 10. Atlanta SBL Press, 2015.

Bowersock, G. W. "An Arabian Trinity." *Harvard Theological Review* 79 (1986) 17–21.

Brown, Francis, et al. *A Hebrew and English Lexicon of the Old Testament*. 1906. Reprint, Oxford: Clarendon, 1978.

Brown, Norman O. *Apocalypse and/or Metamorphosis*. Berkeley: University of California Press, 1991.

Bukhārī, Muḥammad ibn Ismāʿīl. *Sahih Bukhari*. Vol. 6. Translated by M. Muhsin Khan. Edited by Mika'il al-Almany. 8 vols. PDF created and last modified in 2009. Distributed by Islam House. https://d1.islamhouse.com/data/en/ih_books/single/en_Sahih_Al-Bukhari.pdf/.

Burton, J. "Abrogation." In *EQ* 1:11–19.

---

1. Entries for articles from McAuliffe, ed., *Encyclopedia of the Qur'an*. 6 vols. Leiden: Brill, 2006, abbreviate the encyclopedia title as *EQ*.

―――. "Those Are the High Flying Cranes." *Journal of Semitic Studies* 15 (1970) 246–65.

Camp, Claudia V. *Wisdom and the Feminine in the Book of Proverbs.* Bible and Literature Series 11. Sheffield: Almond, 1985.

Campo, Juan Eduardo. "Cave." In *EQ* 1:292–94.

Caskel, Werner, and Gert Strenziok. *Ǧamharat an-Nasasb: Das geneologische Werk des Hišam Ibn Muḥammad al-Kalbī.* Vol. 1. Leiden: Brill, 1966.

Chabbi, Jacqueline. "Jinn." In *EQ* 3:43–49.

―――. "Whisper." In *EQ* 5:478–80.

Charles, R. H., et al., eds. *The Apocrypha and Pseudepigrapha of the Old Testament in English.* Vol. 1, *The Apocrypha.* Oxford: Clarendon, 1913.

Cook, David. "The Prophet Muhammad, Labīd Al-Yahūdī and the Commentaries to Sūra 113." *Journal of Semitic Studies* 45 (2000) 323–45.

Crenshaw, James L. *Old Testament Wisdom: An Introduction.* Rev. ed. Louisville: Westminster John Knox, 1998.

―――. *A Whirlpool of Torment: Israelite Traditions of God as an Oppressive Presence.* Overtures to Biblical Theology 12. Philadelphia: Fortress, 1984.

Crone, Patricia. "The Religion of the Qur'anic Pagans: God and the Lesser Deities." *Arabica* 2 (2010) 151–200.

Cunial, Stefania. "Spiritual Beings." In *EQ* 5:117–21.

Dawood, N. J. trans. *The Koran.* London: Penguin, 1956.

Denny, Frederick Mathewson. "Hand(s)." In *EQ* 2:401–402.

Donner, Fred M. "Reflections on the History and Evolution of Western Study of the Qur'an, from ca. 1900 to the Present." In *New Trends in Qur'anic Studies: Text, Context, and Interpretation,* edited by Mun'im Sirry, 21–45. International Qur'anic Studies Association Studies in the Qur'an 2. Atlanta: Lockwood, 2019.

Droge, A. J., trans. *The Qur'an: A New Annotated Translation.* Comparative Islamic Studies. Sheffield: Equinox, 2013.

Fabri, H. J. "*rab.*" In *Theological Dictionary of the Old Testament,* edited by G. Johannes Botterweck, et al. 13:272–78. Translated by Geoffrey W. Bromiley. Grand Rapids: Eerdmans, 2004.

Faris, Nabih Amin. *The Book of Idols: Being a Translation from the Arabic of the Kitāb Al-Asnam by Hisham Ibn-Al-Kalbi.* Princeton Oriental Studies 14. Princeton: Princeton University Press, 1952.

Fatani, Afnan H. "The Lexical Transfer of Arabic Non-Core Lexicon: Sura 113 of the Qur'an–Al-Falaq (the Splitting)." *Journal of Qur'anic Studies* 4/2 (2002) 61–81.

Freud, Sigmund. *Moses and Monotheism.* Translated by Katherine Jones. Religion and Psychology. New York: Vintage, 1967.

Gade, Anna M. "Recitation of the Qur'an." In *EQ* 4:367–85.

Girard, René. *Deceit, Desire, and the Novel: Self and Other in Literary Structure.* Translated by Yvonne Freccero. Baltimore: Johns Hopkins University Press, 1965.

Gonzalez, Valérie. "Sheba." In *EQ* 4:585–87.

Gordon, Cyrus H. "The Daughters of Baal and Allah." *Moslem World* 33/1 (1943) 50–51.

Guidi, Ignazio. "Seven Sleepers." In *Encyclopedia of Religion and Ethics,* edited by James Hastings, 11:428–30. 13 vols. Edinburgh: T. & T. Clark, 1926.

Gunther, Sebastian. "Days, Times of." In *EQ* 1:499–504.

Harrison, Robert Pogue. "The Prophet of Envy." *New York Review of Books* 65/20 (December 20, 2018) 62–64.

Hawting, G. R. *The Idea of Idolatry and the Emergence of Islam: From Polemic to History.* Cambridge Studies in Islamic Civilization. Cambridge: Cambridge University Press, 1999.

————. "Pre-Islamic Arabia and the Qur'an." In *EQ* 2:253–61.

Hoffman, Valerie J. "Intercession." In *EQ* 2:551–55.

Horst, Pieter W., van der. "Pious Long-Sleepers in Greek, Jewish, and Christian Antiquity." *Studies in Ancient Judaism, and Early Christianity* 87 (2014) 248–66.

Ikwan, Munirul. "Interpreting the Qur'an between Shari'a and Changing Custom: On Women's Dress in Indonesia." In *New Trends in Qur'anic Studies: Text, Context, and Interpretation*, edited by Mun'im Sirry, 211–31. International Qur'anic Studies Association Studies in the Qur'an 2. Atlanta: Lockwood, 2019.

Juynboll, G. H. A. "Hadith and the Qur'an." In *EQ* 2:376–96.

Kahn, Gabriel Mandel. "Magic." In *EQ*, 3:245–51.

Kaltner, John. *Inquiring of Joseph: Getting to Know a Biblical Character through the Qur'an.* Interfaces. Collegeville, MN: Liturgical, 2003.

————. *Ishmael Instructs Isaac: An Introduction the Qur'an for Bible Readers.* Collegeville, MN: Liturgical, 1999.

Lang, Bernhard. *Wisdom and the Book of Proverbs: A Hebrew Goddess Redefined.* New York: Pilgrim, 1986.

Lassner, Jacob. "Bilqis." In *EQ* 1:228–29.

————. *Demonizing the Queen of Sheba: Boundaries of Gender and Culture in Postbiblical Judaism and Medieval Islam.* Chicago Studies in the History of Judaism. Chicago: University of Chicago Press, 1993.

————. "The 'One Who Had Knowledge of the Book' and the 'Mightiest Names of God': Qur'anic Exegesis and Jewish Cultural Artifacts." In *Medieval and Modern Perspectives on Muslim-Jewish Relations,* edited by Ronald L. Nettler, 1:57–74. 2 vols. Studies in Muslim-Jewish Relations 2. Luxembourg: Harwood Academic, 1993.

Leaman, Oliver "Bilqis." In *The Qur'an: An Encyclopedia*, edited by Oliver Leaman, 120–25. London: Routledge, 2006.

————. "Hud-Hud." In *The Qur'an: An Encyclopedia*, edited by Oliver Leaman, 272–74. London: Routledge, 2006.

L'Hopital, Jean-Yves. "Prayer Formulas." In *EQ* 4:231–34.

Ma'mar, Ibn Rāshid. "The Story of the Companions of the Cave." In *The Expeditions: An Early Biography of Muhammad*, 103–5. Translated by Joseph E. Lowrey. Library of Arabic Literature. New York: New York University Press, 2015.

Massignon, Louis. "Le Culte Liturgique Et Populaire des VII Dormants Martyrs d'Ephese (Ahl Al-Kahf)." In *Opera Minora*, 3:119–80. 3 vols. Recherches et documents. Beirut: Dar al-Ma'arif, 1963.

Maududi, Sayyid Abul A'la. *Towards Understanding the Qur'an.* Vol. 7. Translated and edited by Zafar Ishaq Ansari. 14 vols. Leicester, UK: Islamic Foundation, 1998.

McAuliffe, Jane Dammen, ed. *Encyclopaedia of the Qur'an.* 5 vols. Leiden: Brill, 2001–2006.

Mir, Mustansir. "Islāhī's Concept of Sura-Pairs." *Muslim World* 73 (1983) 22–32.

————. "The Names of the Qur'an." In *EQ* 3:505–14.

Nasr, Seyyed Hossein. "Nature as Signs." In *EQ* 3:528–35.

Nasr, Seyyed Hossein, et al., eds. *The Study Quran: A New Translation and Commentary.* New York: HarperOne, 2015.

Netton, Ian Richard. "Towards a Modern Tafsīr of Sūrat-al-Kahf: Structure and Semiotics." *Journal of Qurʾanic Studies* 2/1 (2000) 67–87.

Neuwirth, Angelika. "Form and Structure of the Qurʾan." In *EQ* 2:245–66.

———. "Myths and Legends in the Qurʾān." In *EQ* 3:477–97.

Nibley, Hugh. "Qumran and the Companions of the Cave." *Revue de Qumran* 5 (1965) 177–98.

Nöldeke, Theodor. "Arabs (Ancient)." In *Encyclopedia of Religion and Ethics*, edited by James Hastings, 1:659–73. 13 vols. Edinburgh: T. & T. Clark, 1926.

Obermann, Julian. "Two Elijah Stories in Judea-Arabic Transmission." *Hebrew Union College Annual* 23 (1950) 387–404.

Padwick, Constance E. *Muslim Devotions.* London: Oneworld, 1961.

Paret, R. "Ashab Al-Kahf." In *The Encyclopedia of Islam*, 1:691. 12 vols. Leiden: Brill, 1960.

Penchansky, David. *The Betrayal of God: Ideological Conflict in Job.* Literary Currents in Biblical Interpretation. Louisville: Westminster John Knox, 1990.

———. "Hosea." In *The Jerome Biblical Commentary for the Twenty-First Century*, edited by John J. Collins et al. 3rd, rev. ed. London: Bloomsbury, forthcoming.

———. "Polytheism." In *Vocabulary for the Study of Religion*, edited by Robert Segal and Kocku von Stuckrad, 3:n.p. 3 vols. Leiden: Brill, 2015.

———. "A Qurʾanic Theodicy: Moses in the *Surat al-Kahf* (Q 18)." In *New Trends in Qurʾanic Studies: Text, Context, and Interpretation,* edited by Munʾim Sirry, 95–108. International Qurʾanic Studies Association Studies in the Qurʾān 2. Atlanta: Lockwood, 2019.

———. *Twilight of the Gods: Polytheism in the Hebrew Bible.* Louisville: Westminster John Knox, 2005.

———. *Understanding Wisdom Literature: Conflict and Dissonance in the Hebrew Text.* Grand Rapids: Eerdmans, 2012.

———. *What Rough Beast? Images of God in the Hebrew Bible.* Louisville: Westminster John Knox, 1999.

Pickthall, Marmaduke. *The Glorious Koran: An Explanatory Translation.* New York: Knopf, 1909.

Power, Edmond. "The Prehistory of Islam." *Studies: An Irish Quarterly Review* 2/7 (1913) 204–21.

Pregill, Michael E. "The Hebrew Bible and the Quran: The Problem of the Jewish 'Influence' on Islam." *Religion Compass* 1 (2007) 643–59.

Radscheit, Mathias. "Provocation." In *EQ* 4:308–14.

Raven, Wim. "Reward and Punishment." In *EQ* 4:451–61.

Renard, John. "Khaḍir/khiḍe." In *EQ* 3:81–83.

Reynolds, Gabriel Said. *The Qurʾan and the Bible: Text and Commentary.* Translated by Ali Quli Qaraʾi. New Haven: Yale University Press, 2018.

Rippin, Andrew. "Abū Lahab." In *EQ* 1:20.

———, ed. *The Blackwell Companion to the Qurʾān.* Blackwell Companions to Religion. Oxford: Wiley-Blackwell, 2006.

Roberts, Nancy N. "A Parable of Blessing: The Significance and Message of the Qurʾanic Account of 'the Companions of the Cave.'" *Muslim World* 83 (1993) 295–317.

Robin, Christian Julien. "Les Filles de Dieu." *Semitica* 30 (2001) 113–92.

———. "South Arabia, Religions in Pre-Islamic." In *EQ* 5:84–94.

Robinson, Chase F. "Reconstructing Early Islam: Truth and Consequences." In *Method and Theory in the Study of Islamic Origins,* edited by Herbert Berg, 101–34. Islamic History and Civilization 49. Leiden: Brill, 2003.

Rubin, Uri. "Quraysh." In *EQ* 4:329–33.

Saeed, Abdullah. "Reading the Qur'an Contextually: Approaches and Challenges." In *New Trends in Qur'anic Studies: Text, Context, and Interpretation,* edited by Mun'im Sirry. International Qur'anic Studies Association Studies in the Qur'an 2. Atlanta: Lockwood, 2019.

Sale, George, trans. *The Koran.* 1734. Reprint, New York: Alden, 1883.

Schöck, Cornelia. "Moses." In *EQ* 3:419–26.

Schöller, Marco. "Opposition to Muhammad." In *EQ* 3:576–80.

Schwartzbaum, Haim. "The Jewish and Moslem Versions of Some Theodicy Legends." *Fabula: Zeitschrift für Erzählforschumg* 3 (1959) 119–69.

Sells, Michael. *Approaching the Qur'an: The Early Revelations.* Ashland, OR: White Cloud, 1999.

Shepard, William E. "Age of Ignorance." In *EQ* 1:37–40.

Silberman, Lou H. "The Queen of Sheba in Judaic Traditions." In *Solomon & Sheba,* edited by James B. Pritchard, 65–84. London: Phaidon, 1974.

Sirry, Mun'im. *New Trends in Qur'anic Studies: Text, Context, and Interpretation.* International Qur'anic Studies Association Studies in the Qur'an 2. Atlanta: Lockwood, 2019.

Soucek, Priscilla. "Solomon." In *EQ* 5:76–78.

Speiser, E. A. "The Epic of Gilgamesh." In *Ancient Near Eastern Texts relating to the Old Testament,* edited by James B. Pritchard, 72–99. Princeton: Princeton University Press, 1950.

Stewart, Devin J. "Curse." In *EQ* 2:491.

———. "Soothsayer." In *EQ* 5:78–80.

Tottoli, Roberto. "Men of the Cave." In *EQ* 1:374–75.

———. "Raqim." In *EQ* 1:351–52.

Waines, David. "Date Palm." In *EQ* 1:494–95.

———. "Trees." In *EQ,* 5:358–62.

Waldman, M. "New Approaches to 'Biblical' Materials in the Qur'an." *Muslim World* 75 (1985) 1–16.

Wansbrough, John. *Quranic Studies: Sources and Methods of Scriptural Interpretation.* Amherst, NY: Prometheus, 2004.

Watt, W. Montgomery. "The Queen of Sheba in Islamic Tradition." In *Solomon & Sheba,* edited by James B. Pritchard, 85–103. London: Phaidon, 1974.

Welch, Alford T. "Allah and Other Supernatural Beings: The Emergence of the Qur'anic Doctrine of *Tawḥid.*" *Journal of the American Academy of Religion Thematic Studies* 47 (1979) 733–58.

Wheeler, Brannon M. "The Jewish Origins of Qur'an 18:65–82? Reexamining Arent Jan Wensinck's Theory." *Journal of the American Oriental Society* 118 (1998) 153–71.

———. *Moses in the Qur'an and Islamic Exegesis.* RoutledgeCurzon Studies in the Quran. London: Routledge, 2002.

Wiederhold, Lutz. "Morning." In *EQ* 3:416–19.

Winnett, F. V. "The Daughters of Allah." *Muslim World* 30 (1940) 113–30.

Subject and Author Index

Ancient Document Index